ETHAN DONATI

No One's Coming

From Social Anxiety to Million Dollar Speaker

First published by Ethan Donati Enterprises 2022

Copyright © 2022 by Ethan Donati

All rights reserved. No part of this publication may be reproduced, stored or transmitted in any form or by any means, electronic, mechanical, photocopying, recording, scanning, or otherwise without written permission from the publisher. It is illegal to copy this book, post it to a website, or distribute it by any other means without permission.

Ethan Donati has no responsibility for the persistence or accuracy of URLs for external or third-party Internet Websites referred to in this publication and does not guarantee that any content on such Websites is, or will remain, accurate or appropriate.

Designations used by companies to distinguish their products are often claimed as trademarks. All brand names and product names used in this book and on its cover are trade names, service marks, trademarks and registered trademarks of their respective owners. The publishers and the book are not associated with any product or vendor mentioned in this book. None of the companies referenced within the book have endorsed the book.

First edition

ISBN: 978-0-6455244-0-6

No One's Coming

No one's coming to save you

No one's coming to do it for you

No one's coming to win for you

No one's coming to make you feel better

No one's coming to make sure that you do the work, that you stop procrastinating or that you turn off the TV

No one's coming to create your dream life for you or to achieve your goals for you

It's up to you

It's all up to you.

So what's it going to be? Continue to hide in the shadows, or take your rightful place on the world's stage?

Contents

Foreword	ii
Preface	v

I   My Path to Platform Speaking

1	What is Platform Speaking?	3
2	The Social Anxiety	8
3	Momentum	35
4	Unstoppable Acceleration : The Student Begins Ascension	46
5	From Failure to Winning	54
6	The Year of Dreams	70
7	The Play by Play	74

II   The Stage is Yours

8	Your Stage Is Set	99
9	The Magician Reveals His Tricks	101
10	Produce Events Like A Pro	103
11	What To Sell As A Speaker	115
12	How To Put Butts In Seats	147
13	Speak Your Way To Millions	163
14	The Step By Step Masterplan Sequence	183
15	It's Your Turn	207

About the Author	210

Foreword

This is the real story of a young man who undertook a tough journey from reclusive shyness to world domination.

An ordinary story about an extraordinary metamorphosis.

Success is often the result of a personal journey of sacrifice. Ethan's story chronicles a particularly challenging start, and the sacrifices which lead him to victory.

As a master certified business coach, a speaker coach and a master certified sales coach, I work with entrepreneurs, speakers, start ups, and business owners all over the world.

Ethan Donati attended a business coaching event in Sydney, Australia. He was only 23 years old.

He painfully stumbled through his 30 second introduction, and barely said a word throughout the entire four day event.

Ethan Donati suffered from crippling shyness. The mere thought of speaking, being looked at, or being put in the spotlight, was a challenge of monumental proportions for him.

As an intensely introverted business owner, it was almost impossible to imagine Ethan ever being able to lead a team, pitch his product, or motivate an audience. Playing the role of rainmaker in his business was unimaginable.

Simply put, Ethan Donati was a challenging client for any business coach.

The real obstacle in Ethan's business growth was his inability to communicate on any verbal level.

But, anyone can learn to speak publicly, I kept telling myself, even despite a crippling social disability.

And so, the work began across two continents. I tasked Ethan with creating an initial presentation which would articulate the benefits, value and outcomes of his service.

We crafted an irresistible offer and wove around it a robust call to action.

We discussed seeding, objection handling, bonuses and benefit stacks for hours on end, until Ethan understood the anatomy of a perfect close.

Ethan delivered that presentation over and over to an audience of one. I was in South Africa, and he was in Melbourne. A lone audience member sales coach, with a determined young speaker and future salesman extraordinaire.

Warren Buffet once said "My public speaking course was arguably the best investment I made in my life"

This quote is so true of Ethan Donati.

Often the greatest business challenges are blessings as they force us to sharpen the axe.

Ethan set about the sharpening process with absolute determination.

He was relentless in his pursuit of success. His determination to overcome his greatest challenge became greater than the challenge itself.

Fast forward a few short years. Ethan is now 27 years old.

He is an internationally acclaimed platform and stage speaker.

Ethan promotes sold out seminars, all over the world. He is a keynote speaker, a remarkable closer and a brilliant event promoter. Celebrities often share the stage with Ethan at his sold out events.

Ethan was selected to present a TEDx talk.

He has twice been awarded the coveted two comma club award, for earning a million dollars out of a single marketing funnel.

In April last year after working with Ethan once again on his presentation and his call to action, he went on to earn a million dollars in a single week of speaking at three events.

If Ethan turned "Impossible" into "I'm Possible", then anyone who is fortunate enough to be reading this book, can do the same.

Now fasten your seat belts as you devour this page-turning rollercoaster ride into the realm of success.

Ethan, as your speaker coach and your friend, it is a rare privilege to pen the foreword to your extraordinary life story.

Ethan's story doesn't end here. It has just begun

Cherie Eilertsen
Global Speaker Coach.
Master Certified Business Coach, Executive Coach and Sales Coach.

Preface

"Everything negative—pressure, challenges—is all an opportunity for me to rise."

- Kobe Bryant

There were only 3 days until the biggest tour of my life and the insurmountable pressure was taking its toll. My whole body had broken out in what seemed like hives…

I was completely covered with red, itchy spots. I was struggling to breathe and was overheating every couple of hours.

I was supposed to speak in just a couple of days, but not just to speak, it was my event, my name was on the poster, the advertising, the promoting, even the side of the building!

I knew one thing though, I couldn't mess this one up.

I was already $250,000 in.

Yes $250,000.

That's a lot of money for anyone, but as a 26 year old, just a couple years out of university, it was that much more important that this tour paid off.

The day of the first event arrives. I had about 3 hours of sleep due to all of the anxiety and nerves (I am an extreme introvert, so thinking about getting on a stage is daunting at the best of times, let alone getting on a stage after 12 months of being locked away due to covid.) This was the first time I was giving an in person talk in over a year, and the first time I was producing an event on a stage like this.

My body was still a mess, I was spending the morning taking plenty of Telfast and skin creams to try to get some semblance of normalcy before the event. None of it really worked.

Regardless, the show must go on.

I arrived at the venue, it was still surreal to see myself all over the biggest convention center in Melbourne, take a tour of the stage, meet the team and then I was off to the green room.

The green room, all alone, to mull in my thoughts. Maybe not the best idea. I was extremely nervous now so with about 10 minutes before I was due on, I messaged one of my mentors. He replied and video called me, told me to chill out and reminded me that I have already done all the hard work and now it was time to share that to inspire the audience. Some will like it, some will hate it and that's ok. My nerves started to go down, I rushed onto the stage, the lights were on and it's…. SHOWTIME.

Most speakers just give a speech and leave. But that's not how the speaking business works if you actually want to be a profitable speaker. The best speakers make an offer to the audience. And like I said, I was $250,000 in, there had to be a way to turn that risk into a profit.

The presentation was fine and it was now time to make an offer at about the 90 minute mark.

I went to go and play the most important video testimonial of my whole presentation.

I click the play button.

White screen.

I go back and try again.

White screen...

SHIT! The video wasn't uploaded properly to the presentation. The most crucial time of the whole presentation and this is the mistake I have made?

I act like it's normal and continue.

I make the offer, tell them to go to the back to buy...

No one is moving...

It feels like forever... still no one is buying, no one is going to the back of the room.

Has everything been for nothing?

No One's Coming

Why did I call it that? Because nothing could be truer.

What I find is that most people simply blame others or their circumstances for not achieving what they want. They stay in complacency waiting for 'someone else to do it'.

No one else is going to do it for you, no one cares more than you if you achieve anything in life.

Stop watching life go by and actually seize the mantle, take control of where you end up, take control of what is going on and snap out of your autopilot daze that the modern world has you in.

This book may just change the trajectory of your life. I know that when I learned and implemented what I have included in this book, mine definitely changed.

I went from suffering crippling social anxiety, barely able to speak to even close friends and family, into an international speaker, speaking in front of up to 3,000 complete strangers at once and earning more in a single presentation than most people do in a year.

Now I am the go to marketer and funnel builder for speakers, personal brands and coaches alike. I have had the pleasure of working with and alongside celebrities and I have been responsible for running the marketing machine behind 7 and 8 figure entrepreneurs, using these exact same methods that I will show you.

This book will start off with a detailed look into my own personal transformation and the personal development lessons that I had to learn to make the new version of me into a reality. My intention is that by sharing this, it will inspire you and even give you the confidence that you need to get over whatever may be holding you back. I went from a complete loser with no friends, extremely socially awkward to a world class closer and international speaker. If there is one key lesson to give you from the start, it is the same one I delivered in my TEDx talk: your biggest perceived weakness will propel you to the top. You just need to embrace it instead of hiding from it.

Part of me does not really want to write this, because no doubt copycats will start popping up. However the lessons, steps and advice are too powerful to keep hidden. I don't believe there is another book on speaking like this on the market, and there is no one that will truly show you their numbers and reveal the magic behind the curtain like I am about to.

This skill set and this industry have largely been kept secret.

Until now…

Let me introduce you to the world of platform speaking.

The first time I ever came across 'platform speaking' was at an event I attended when I was about 18 years old to see one of my idols, Eric Thomas 'ET'. The speaker before him did something I had never seen any speaker do. He made an offer to the audience. The thing is, no one was there to see him, we were there to see ET. This other speaker was speaking just before ET went on stage. He was a platform speaker invited by the promoter so that the event could make a profit. Watching this in real time I was so confused but also in awe as to what was happening.

From memory the price was about $4,000, and I thought who in the world is going to go and buy this thing from some random guy that no one knows? Well to my surprise people just kept popping up. One, two, three, fifteen, twenty. I was doing the math in my head, that speaker made at least $150,000, maybe $200,000 in under two hours and no one knew him before that day!

I thought to myself, how is this possible?

Well little did I know, about 8 years later I would be that speaker. I earned $1.3 million in 7 days with just 3 events at 26 years old, and what did I realize? It really wasn't that hard (and I am not even a good speaker).

When I first saw that platform speaker at the Eric Thomas event (who I later went onto befriend and do business with, Aaron Sansoni), I did not actually have a business, I didn't even have an idea of what business I wanted to start, but I always knew I was destined for more, I always had this burning fire within me to achieve things that very few people ever would.

I built a tremendous amount of tenacity and resilience in my early life because of how socially 'strange' I was and how hard it was for me to even make one friend. This gave me a fire that most never get to truly experience. In some regards they are the lucky ones, they get to live a normal life and be satisfied by normal life things. In some regards I am the lucky one, I get to push myself and reach heights that very few ever will. It just depends on what your goals are in life.

When I saw what was possible with speaking, I thought that it could be an avenue for me. Not straight away of course, I had a lot of personal development growth to go through first. But eventually I thought this may be my 'end game'.

If you have never considered speaking as a form of wealth or career path for you, I challenge you to keep your mind open. Chances are you are probably more equipped to become a speaker than I was at the beginning. Allow yourself to be disrupted and confronted by the thought or possibility that this business model could be the one for you.

There is no other form of wealth or business model that I have ever seen in my life where someone could go and make $200,000 in a day. My parents always instilled the belief in me that $100,000 in a year was an incredible salary. This blew my mind at the time, how is it possible then that people can make a year's salary in a couple of hours? Imagine all the spare time you would have to do whatever you want if you could simply achieve a year's salary in a day is what I thought to myself.

The major issue was that I had crippling social anxiety so it wasn't just as easy as making a speech and having a go. There are so many moving parts and nuances to this skill and I will share as many as I can within this book. It took me about 3 years of being in business before I even tried speaking.

Everything that I did before becoming a speaker helped me be even better by the time I stood on the stage for the first time. So when you read this, it isn't only the end destination that I want you to focus on, it's all the steps and nuances in between that you want to pay close attention to.

This book isn't necessarily only a 'How To', it's a combination of things - the lessons, the principles, the stories of how I did it and to finish I will give you the steps to create a powerful presentation yourself.

The truth is, there is no blanket 'how to' because everyone's way to get to this level of speaking or the top in any industry is vastly different. Yes there are some universal principles anyone can apply to get a base level of results, but your way of getting to those results will most likely be different to anyone else's.

One part I am not going to cover in depth is the marketing part, I have many resources on that elsewhere, and if you want to work with me directly, go to my website: www.ethandonati.com.

I

My Path to Platform Speaking

1

What is Platform Speaking?

P latform speaking isn't for the faint of heart, I'll tell you that. If just 10% of the audience enjoys your presentation you can be a millionaire in a week or even a day depending on the size of your audience. Yes, that means that maybe 90% of the audience won't absolutely love you so if you're someone that needs to be liked by everyone, well you're in trouble. But you see, most speakers are dead broke because they focus on the applause and not on the credit card. Sounds harsh, but you'll see what I mean as I explain all of the different ways to think about this.

Platform speaking is the opposite of what you probably think a speaker is. The speaker that you probably think of is what's called a 'Keynote Speaker'. A keynote speaker gets paid by someone else and they get paid for their time. For example a school or a university might hire you to do a presentation, you speak for an hour or 30 minutes and you give a talk, everyone applauds, you get your cheque, and you leave. Simple, easy, no fuss, but also little to no money unless you are a celebrity. It is hard to make a living like that if you are not someone in the public eye. You don't really know where and when your next gig is coming from, you don't know who is hiring you, and you rely on someone else to make your economy for you. Plus you're getting paid for time. Sooner or later everyone runs out of time. A keynote speaker trades time for money. A platform speaker gets paid for results, there is an uncapped amount of money you could make with your time in this business model. You are only capped by the amount of people in the audience and the price of what you are offering.

Don't get me wrong, keynote speaking is great for building your personal brand. For example I have given a TEDx talk before which is a keynote, but you should not rely on keynotes as your source of income. Still do them by all means, but that can't be your strategy to hit your first or next million as a speaker.

Platform speaking is essentially the complete opposite of keynote speaking. You get paid for the results you create instead of the time you spend… and no one has to know who you are. You can even make your own events (more on this later), and don't need to rely on someone paying you a wage or fee. You create your own economy. A platform speaker goes on stage to sell a solution to the audience and you get paid depending on how many people buy what you are selling. When you get paid for results, the sky's the limit, your earning potential is uncapped and you can start realistically dreaming big.

I'm not talking about selling a $20 book or a low ticket product, I am talking about selling something for $3,000-$5,000, even higher. Let's say you have a $3,000 product or service and 20 people buy it. You've just earned $60,000 in one presentation. The only people that can command that kind of money for a keynote presentation are celebrities. Now let's say you do that twice a month for a year. That is a $120,000/month or $1,440,000 per year speaking business. Not too bad if you ask me.

Welcome to the world of platform speaking.

Sounds like a get rich quick scam? Well the truth is that there is a lot that goes behind the 2 hour presentation, the years, hours, sleepless nights that make it look like you can become an overnight success in one presentation.

WHAT IS PLATFORM SPEAKING?

It's like the Usain Bolt analogy:

Usain Bolt has only spent 325 seconds on the Olympics track. He has earned an Olympic Gold Medal every 36 seconds that he has been on the track. It was worked out that he earns over $1 million per second when he competes. But it took him 20 years to get there.

So yes, platform speaking can make you a lot of money in a short amount of time, but where most people think it seems like a get rich quick opportunity, the truth is there are many factors that you need to master before you even get ON the stage let alone convert that into a six or seven figure day.

And I will share something that Myron Golden shared to my audience; You better hope it's a get rich quick opportunity, because the real scam is getting rich slowly.

I couldn't agree more, getting rich slowly sucks. It's actually easier to make more money in less time. Seriously. It's easier to make one million in a week than it is to make it in a year. I hope this blows your mind as much as it did mine the first time I was hearing this.

Sound too good to even be believable, to even believe that you could make $100,000 in a couple of hours? I thought so too.

But if I can do it, anyone can.

If I can do it, so can you.

A lot of people say 'if I can do it, so can you' but often they haven't really gone through the experiences required to confidently say that. I have though and that's why I am so confident that with a little bit of focus and coaching that almost anyone can become a successful platform speaker. Very few ever will though. It is probably one of the hardest skills to master in the business world, not to mention that the biggest fear in the world is public speaking too.

For me that's what made it more attractive. If so few ever even have a go let alone master it, imagine if you could? Imagine if you could just get kinda good and not even need to master it. That's how my brain works. Find out what most people never even realistically dream of doing, and let me go and do that.

> *"There's a thousand you's, there's only one of me"*
> *- Kanye West, Stronger*

Most people never become the speaker, and it's pretty simple to prove this. Go to any event. How many speakers are there compared to how many people in the crowd attending? There may be 1-5 speakers and 100-10,000 people in the audience. There's your answer. Want to achieve the results of the few? Then you need to be in the 1-5 number not in the 100-10,000 number!

Most people spend their time consuming content. Getting their little dopamine burst from sharing the next motivational quote like that's going to change their life or their behavior. It's pure virtue signaling. Get a grip. If you aren't acting like it, don't tell me about it until you actually go and do the thing. You have people talking about 'grinding' and wanting success and all this kind of high achiever stuff, but then these same people are the ones staying up all night watching Netflix, sulking when the first thing goes wrong, partying all the time or giving up after an average or below average start. I love entrepreneurs, I really do but jeez sometimes we need to honestly get a grip and have some perspective.

I truly believe the biggest roadblock to why most people don't ever achieve their desired outcome is themselves. They have the wrong environment, lack discipline, eat the wrong food, hang out with the wrong crowd, can't control their social media or Netflix addiction, don't spend nearly enough time strategically on their business and the biggest one - failure to think logically or see things as part of a bigger picture and instead act emotionally, without rationality and seek immediate gratification. Most also don't have enough pain, therefore lacking the desire to overcome the pain and are instead comfortable and complacent which means they don't have the level of drive required to be successful.

And then you have the other side of the spectrum of people believing that they can watch 'The Secret', or just 'build it and they will come', think positively, manifest their dream life, wait for a divine intervention, read some new book about success and brag how they ready 25 books a week and that everything will magically fall into place like a fairytale. Give me a break. It takes actual work, resilience, skill and commitment, everything else is a distraction to prevent you from actually achieving the goal you want to achieve in the first place. Because it's easier to say 'I tried a little bit and it didn't work' than it is to put 100% of yourself into something and face the fact you may still actually fail. But I tell you what, at least you will know and you won't have to lie to yourself. Put your whole self in for once, and if you fail fine, but you actually might succeed…

2

The Social Anxiety

For me I never had an issue with pain, drive or motivation. Firstly motivation is bullshit, no one is 100% motivated every single day, discipline is infinitely more important. I can't believe the amount of people that attend events and the reason they write down for attending is 'so I can get motivated & inspired.' Are you kidding me? I'm sorry but if you are not already motivated and inspired then business is not for you, get a job, quit, retire, do anything else. If you blame motivation for your shortcomings, it's time for some real deep life chats with yourself.

Back to the drive and motivation. Now for me I've always had this deeply ingrained in everything that I do. I am an extremely competitive individual. This has helped me but it can also alienate people too. Like I said, if you are a people pleaser or you need to be liked by everyone, this industry may not be the best idea for you.

The underlying driving factor to this motivation and drive though was the immense pain that I had to go through emotionally and mentally for basically all of my life. The pain was brought on from my debilitating social anxiety. This is why I am confident when I say that if I can do this, you can too. I'm not talking about being a little bit shy, I'm talking about not saying a word, to anyone, even family or friends, and being the weird kid who didn't say anything. All my life. I couldn't make friends, couldn't speak up for myself, couldn't put myself out there. And it wasn't just when I was young, no this literally stayed with me until 22 years old. You could argue that I still have it, to a lesser degree, now in fact.

My best friend throughout my whole childhood was basically my cousin Andrea. She was essentially the only person I could confide in. In fact when I was maybe 12 years old I remember that she wrote me a card for my birthday and in it said 'can't wait to grow old together with you'. That was really the first time I felt that someone else on this Earth actually cared about me. So much so that I still remember that card to this day. Apart from her, I really had no one else I spoke to.

Anyone that knows me prior to 2019 can tell you their stories about how awkward I was (some may say, still am) and you will see their perspective about how immense that transformation has been. I was really a lost cause.

Here are some quotes from people who knew me prior to who I am today:

Patty Duque, she met me in 2018 when I attended my first ever business event:

"I met Ethan when he was a complete introvert, and he could barely look at me in the eye. And it's not because it was me, he would not look at anyone in the eye. He was so shy it was unbelievable. Seriously he is the real deal, I'm not kidding, because I met him when he was like hiding. I love what you have created in the last 2-3 years, from this little voice, to who you are now, congratulations."

Jos Kasperczyk, met through working at the tennis in 2014:

"I worked with Ethan for 3 or 4 years, and I don't think I heard him say a single word. Something must have switched in his head and he just... took off."

NO ONE'S COMING

Reggie Batts, met through a business event in 2018:

"I'll never forget the day I met you. You were as frightened as a kid being dropped off at a new school. But, you pushed through and now you're living your best life. I'm proud of you."

I mean I got kicked out of kindergarten at 3 years old after day 1 for being 'too shy'. They genuinely took my mum aside after the first day and they told her not to bring me back to kindergarten because I was too shy and didn't talk to anyone.

There is another memory I have when I was in prep. We were told to read a book after we finished our work. Yet after I finished I was too nervous to get out of my seat and get up in front of everyone to even go get a book. I waited for permission from my teacher who ended up getting a little bit stern. Then in grade 1 in a class activity, the teacher asked a question: "what type of vehicle would transport a brick?" She chose someone at random to answer in front of everyone. I would sweat and pray I would never be asked. This time she did ask me and I freaked out and said "plane." The whole classroom laughed. I tried to laugh as well to make it seem like it was normal but the embarrassment I felt that day is something that I have felt quite often. The fact I even remember these silly moments illustrate how much I struggled since a very young age with this.

This behavior stayed with me all my life, I remember graduating high school and barely having any friends and not being able to even talk to anyone. University was the same, I was too nervous to even attend classes sometimes and ended up failing three subjects in my first year!

This pain of being unable to make friends or communicate for literally 20+ years was what started the drive. It was debilitating and I experienced that pain every single day, all day. I couldn't make friends let alone talk to a girl to find a partner. The biggest issue I had was that I couldn't start or hold a conversation, I wasn't interesting, I was always nervous wondering what if someone talks to me, what would I say? Would I be able to hold a conversation?

Even during family get-togethers for events like Christmas or Easter that most people look forward to were a nightmare for me. They were probably the most anxiety ridden events for me because they were all day, lots of people and anything could happen socially. I couldn't even ask my aunties or cousins to pass over a glass of water at the Christmas table for example. If we were one on one I was fine, but it was the pressure of everyone else watching and listening to me. What if I sounded awkward or weird in front of everyone. The embarrassment was something I struggled with and wanted to avoid at all costs.

If stories like these aren't giving you hope at your own possibilities, I don't know what will.

This constant pain and discomfort created what's called 'petty motivation'. Which basically means I was motivated by outdoing other what I considered 'socially normal' people in other areas of life. For the longest time I put this motivation into sport - specifically tennis. And then this later transmuted into business and wealth. One of my first mentors, Owen Cook, breaks down motivation in 3 categories: Higher Self Motivation - motivated by achievements that transcend yourself, such as legacy. Middle Self Motivation - motivated by achievements that give you tangible things like a nice house or car, holidays and then Lower Self Motivation - motivated by petty things, like beating someone else in something or showing someone who doubted you that they were wrong. If you watch the 'Last Dance' you'll see Michael Jordan also heavily relied on Lower Self Motivation at times in his career. The truth is you may use all three levels differently for different times, but for me the lower self, petty motivation, really got me going.

This pain also forced me to do two things. Firstly it forced me to become interesting. If I was interesting I thought maybe people would talk to me and start the conversation with me, which was easier than me starting the conversation with them. I also had this belief that if I was asking people questions about themselves that this was me being nosy or intrusive so I didn't know how to start or hold a conversation. Secondly, it forced me to want to fix the problem. So I learned social skills. Sounds weird I know, but this should be giving you confidence. If I had to learn social skills because of how awkward I was and I ended up becoming a speaker, what's your excuse?

How did I learn social skills? Well to be fair, I wanted to learn how to be more social so I could talk to girls. I had no idea how to do that, so I did the natural thing and searched on Youtube. I came across a lot more than I expected. The lessons were not only about how to talk to girls, it was about so much more. I learned about deeper inner game principles, self esteem, self worth, core confidence instead of situational confidence, all of these concepts that I didn't even know I needed or existed. I learned about human behavior, why humans behave the way they do, how they think, how we are wired, why we are wired that way and what to do about it. It absolutely fascinated me, I spent at least an hour or two after every school day studying and watching more content.

Some of the social aspects were so foreign to me, topics like 'subcommunication', non verbal communication and being able to pick up on different social cues. For a completely awkward introvert, and perhaps on the spectrum a tiny bit, this also blew my mind, the fact that people communicated in ways other than with words? In fact the words you say only contribute to 7% of communication and that the words they say sometimes don't actually mean what you think they mean or how the person feels? What a puzzling concept it was.

For most people they just take this stuff for granted, but I'm happy that I was never able to. It forced me to learn these principles that not many people take the time to learn, which gave me a deeper understanding of people than most may ever be able to appreciate.

From someone that literally had to learn social skills (yet funnily enough never took a class on how to speak publicly), take it from me, if I can become a speaker, you can too.

The need to win and to win now.

Your next lesson is that you need to move faster, much faster. Patience is a privilege, you don't know how long you're going to live, what right do you have to go slow?

A lot of people are sometimes surprised at the pace I move and how fast I go at times, plus the immense ambition I have had to achieve certain milestones that most may deem unrealistic for my age. And I agree with them, I tend to move very fast and I do achieve results that most are not able to in the timeframes I set myself. It's one thing to set the goal and say what you want in a hopeful sense, but I actually fully believe I can achieve the goal I set myself.

When I was talking to a friend back in year 11 they asked me what do I want to do after I leave school, and I remember saying 'I have no idea but I want to have my own business, be an "entrepreneur" and be a millionaire by 25.' I didn't know how I was going to get there but I knew I wanted to get there and believed I could. It ended up that I would make my first million at 25 but not become a millionaire until 26.

Most people get caught up in the how. "How do I achieve this result?" The how kills dreams. Don't worry about the how first, set the goal, the 'what' and then you'll be surprised how the world works to give you the 'how' when you want something bad enough.

To me though it was never a goal about the money. It was a goal about proving to myself that I could actually achieve something that monumental. I didn't know anyone around me at that time that was thinking differently or that had demonstrated ambition outside of the classroom, let alone actually put in the work it takes to live up to your ambition. I wanted to be different.

This need to win now is partially because I set my measuring stick at a higher bar than most. I don't compare myself to what the average person is doing, I look for someone doing 10x more than me, especially if they are at a younger age than me. That way I know that I am not the best and that I can do better. This also keeps your ego in check and doesn't allow you to get too cocky or too comfortable.

I would advise that you refrain from looking at your immediate circle or comparing yourself to them. Unless they are more ambitious than you or at minimum the same level, then chances are you are going to already be near the top of your circle. Yes it might make you feel good or feel like you've accomplished something, but that is how you kill any drive - satisfaction. Comparing yourself can be a tough thing for a lot of people, because it can make you feel like you are not good enough. Most mainstream advice will tell you to only compare yourself to you, which I do agree with, but at the same time if you have never achieved the goal you want, then you need to have a measuring stick at the very least of someone who has achieved that goal.

It's like the story of the 4 minute mile. It was seemingly impossible, no one could do it. Then one day Roger Bannister broke the 4 minute mile and what do you know? Someone else did, and someone else, and someone else until the point that it became routine or normal. You need a measuring stick, you need to see someone else doing it so that you can rationalize that it is possible. Hold yourself to the higher standard or even better yet, set the standard if you can't find it anywhere else.

That desire and ambition to win now stems from something else that I realized at a young age: we aren't going to live forever. Most people understand this but they don't fully embrace it or they don't think about it. For me I saw my life paved out for me: go to school, uni, get a job, retire at 70 and then enjoy life. I knew that was not for me. I realized this at 11 years old because my grandfather had motor neuron disease. If you don't know what that is, it is perhaps the most debilitating disease in the world. You lose speech, the ability to move, eat, talk, it's horrible. It's also known as ALS, which you may know from the ice bucket challenge.

Regardless, this is what he had, and he passed away shortly thereafter. As an 11 year old being around my grandfather, I was probably exposed to a level of mortality earlier than most. And that's when I said, holy shit, if this is how I am going to end up when I get older I better make the most of every single day whilst I'm younger and enjoy everything that I can.

And that was my grandfather, who was almost 80. Who even says we are going to live until 80? My childhood hero and role mode, Kobe Bryant tragically passed away at 41!

This is why I have the desire to win now, because who knows what is going to happen later? Why should we only enjoy life when we are older? It's not just being aware of your mortality, it's actually understanding that you are mortal. Grim? Perhaps, but it's also immensely freeing.

I think people move too slow, are too complacent and are too comfortable, they play it too safe. No judgment to them either, that's an easier, normal, less stressful life. Sometimes I wish I could be fulfilled by a life like that too, but what's the point of being average when you can be great?

In school you used to be 'cool' if you 'didn't try', I think the most common phrase I heard after we got test results back was, 'oh I didn't even try on this test' like that was supposed to be some badge of honor? Imagine if it was actually cool to try, how much better the world would be.

Another important phrase I remember is 'touch wood'. Looking back this phrase causes more insecurity than maybe any other! People say 'touch wood' after you do something good. For example "wow you are playing so well recently… touch wood' implying that you don't think the good performance can be sustained or that it is a 'fluke'. No wonder people have imposter syndrome and doubt their ability to sustain high performance when they have been taught to doubt themselves from when they were kids with this bullshit "touch wood" phrase.

Our early years are our most formative years that bias how we live the rest of our lives. What things do you remember from your early years that maybe had an incidental effect on how you view the world and even how you view yourself? Why do you believe the things you believe? Why do you move slow and procrastinate when things get harder? It's probably not your fault, just years of conditioning and bad habits cemented into your subconscious. It is your fault if you don't change it though.

Support Groups & Role Models

I believe that support groups and role models do play a vital role especially early in life. They are very different things and not to be confused. We generally overestimate the importance of support groups and underestimate the importance of having strong role models. Anyone can give you support, support is nothing more than nice words and good intentions. A mother can say to a child "at least you tried, better luck next time" a role model would show how you should perform better next time, what tweaks to make. Not necessarily by them telling you to your face, but by them showing you with their actions.

A support group are people that you know and that are around you. These are usually your immediate family and friends. Yes they may say they support you and whatever other comforting words they say when they are directly asked but that is a whole different can of worms to actually assisting you in the achievement of fulfilling your ambition and your desired goal. A support group should not be relied upon, nor be the benchmark for, your success. Especially when they are not driven by the same things that you are driven by, nor want to achieve the things that you want to achieve. In fact, if you're not careful, your immediate support group will actually prevent you from achieving your full potential.

You've probably heard of the line 'you are the average of the 5 people you hang around with the most.' There are truths to that. You do accept different behaviors as 'normal' or as 'true' depending on who you are around the most, especially in those earlier years. These people are your parents, siblings and maybe some close friends. The thing is though that these behaviors you see as acceptable or normal are not usually the behaviors designed to help you achieve your best self. Unless your parents or siblings are already high performing individuals it's very unlikely that they are instilling ambitious beliefs and behaviors in you.

It's not their fault, they don't mean any ill intention and it doesn't mean you have to avoid them. You just need to be wary about what you do and do not listen to. You have to be able to prevent their world views and suggestions of what is best for you from meddling with your mind.

If you find yourself asking "What if I don't want to reach or even try to reach my full potential?" or anything similar, it's a sign that you have been spending too much time with the wrong people. These self doubt thoughts are not you speaking, it is a culmination of other people's self doubts and apathy being projected onto you without you being able to filter them out.

Other common questions or statements from people in this limbo of being influenced by their support group to become more apathetic towards their best self include: "This doesn't feel like me" "I don't think I want to achieve this anymore" "I just want to be happy and fulfilled" "I don't want to be seen or to be famous, I don't need to be in the public eye."

Do you see the problem with all of these statements?

They are all 'me' or 'I' statements. They are *selfish* statements.

Achieving your best self isn't about being famous, or being seen or any other vanity metric for that matter. Do you know why it's important to be your absolute best or at least try to be your best? It's not only for you. It's because when you shine you are giving permission for others to follow in your footsteps.

I don't do this for fame or because I want attention, I do this because I am helping someone who is just like I was. Someone who couldn't speak to people, didn't have any idea how they were going to make it in this world and instead I am giving them the permission and the belief to do something better with their lives. I get to instill the belief in them that they are capable of achieving anything. It doesn't matter how you start, that's not your fault, but it is your fault where you end up. I do this for that person in their room alone, too scared and nervous to get up the next day because they don't feel like they belong.

Stepping into a better version of yourself means that you get to inspire the next person and the next person and the next person. Until you have had someone look up to you I don't think that is an easy idea to comprehend. It's also not easy to comprehend when everyone you look up to, especially as a kid, hasn't delivered on what you thought they would, they haven't lived up to actually being a role model for you. They have failed you, and you are scared you may fail someone else too.

You might inspire someone that you don't even know right now. Or it may even be your kids, heck it could even be your parents. Based on your behavior, what kind of example are you setting for your kids or future kids? Would they see someone who is setting the example of continual self improvement, discipline and drive or would they see someone who isn't reliable, is all over the place and demonstrating apathetic behavior? This is much bigger than you. This is legacy.

You can't inspire anyone remaining a secret, remaining in apathy and convincing yourself that you aren't made for this. Look around you. Are the people that you hang out with inspiring anyone? Are the people that you 'chill' with the kinds of people that you would want your kids to turn out to be or to hang around with?

The truth is that everyone is made for this, but only very few establish the traits and go through the sacrifices required to cause that ripple effect, to inspire others to take their leap of faith and push the boundaries of what they are capable of.

Your success makes you into a role model for others. That kind of responsibility is not for everyone. It's easier to sit back, smoke and drink with your friends. It's easier to numb your mind and ignore it or try to wait for it to just disappear. There comes a time when you need to grow up and realize what served you in the past isn't going to get you to where your best self wants you to be and it definitely won't get you to the place that your past self needs you to be, the place that those who you could inspire need you to be. Step up and take your responsibility instead of shying away from it. Not for you, stop thinking that it is all about your own selfish motivations, it's about those that will rely on you.

The most common excuse I hear is that "this new me isn't the real me." This is just imposter syndrome. It's being comfortable with the status quo and the behaviors we grew up with. I have had the privilege to help many beginners make the transition from 'normal' life to a high performance life. Almost all of them during the more difficult moments hit a success ceiling and a comfort barrier. This is the point where the old self is essentially about to die if you continue along your higher self's journey. The most common phrase that I hear during this time is "I'm not sure if this is what I want, I think I can go back to my normal life and be ok there instead."

It's that comfortable brain talking, it's the temptation brain. It will trick you into thinking you never wanted this, you're better off being comfortable and you're better off playing small. It's like Adam and Eve. You have these temptations trying to take you off the path. Don't fall for them! Look up the study called 'Rat Park', the rats keep pushing the lever to activate their reward and pleasure region in the brain. They keep doing this until they die. They don't eat, they don't sleep, they don't drink, all they care about is to keep pressing that lever for small bursts of dopamine and pleasure. Most people in this world put their immediate gratification over long term success and legacy. Even when they start on a path of success and legacy and then realize what it involves, they then go back to the immediate gratification.

If you honestly think you're better off being your old self and therefore not even trying to reach your best self then remember the story of the elephant and the rope. When the elephants in the circus are small they keep them from running away by tying their leg to a rope. When they get bigger, the elephant is much stronger and can obviously run away. Why don't they? Because when they grow up they still believe that the rope is enough to tie them, so they don't even try. Just because they believe they can't do something and because they are used to the same environment being comfortable, they don't even try!

This is where role models come into it. If you have the right role models you will break through this barrier. If you have the wrong ones, even with a nice support network, you will not break through it.

When we are born our role models and our support network are the same: parents, older siblings, maybe a friend or two, teachers. Unfortunately most people never break the shackles and find new role models and this is why 99% of people do not achieve what they are truly capable of.

These role models dramatically influence your entire life. Some kids get their parents to pay for their car and their university degree and as a result usually fail in key traits and areas that it takes to stand on their own. They lack drive because they get everything handed on a silver platter. A role model makes their kids earn it for themselves.

I've heard more extreme examples of role models abusing or not fully accepting their responsibility. Like an older sibling asking their younger siblings to borrow serious money when they are still kids or an older sibling putting their younger siblings in poor environments surrounded by drugs, alcohol and questionable people. Nothing gets me more upset than someone that is supposed to be a role model yet sets a terrible example for those that look up to them and rely on them. The sad thing is, the person looking up to the role model especially when it is a relative or close friend usually thinks it's ok and accepts it because it's all they have known. Demand better and raise your standards. It's not ok, and they should know that it isn't ok.

Most of your support network doesn't want you to outgrow them, in fact it scares them. Especially if they are lifelong friends and family. The second you start pushing the boundaries, stepping into your better self they either go dead silent or they tell you to come back and tempt you with other crap you don't need. The second you start slipping back into the person that they expect you to be, all of a sudden it's all fine and it's like they never treated you any differently. Wake up!

I was fortunate that my parents were always supportive and had very positive traits. They never handed me anything - they didn't buy me a car, pay for my degree or buy me a house, and that's how it should be. I have had to earn everything and so should you. But they could never be my only role models because they had not achieved what I wanted to achieve.

A role model doesn't need to be someone you know personally, it can be a celebrity or sports star as well. The traits I would recommend you look for in role models and in your support network are: resilience, reliability, discipline, persistence, tenacity and relentless drive.

For me my biggest role model was Kobe Bryant. He not only had all of those traits but he was probably ranked #1 on pretty much all of them at the peak of his powers. It may sound silly, but when you are feeling down and out or uncertain about yourself and then you ask 'What would Kobe do?' there's a whole new level of responsibility and belief as to what you can achieve. When you start behaving in alignment with your role models then your old support network may start to see you as a bit weird, crazy and out there because of how driven you are. That's a sign that you are on the right path.

The story after my schooling years

After completing high school, I went to University (I got in with special consideration plus I was awarded an Elite Athlete Scholarship for Tennis), failed my first year, went back and completed my degree. That same University, The University Of Melbourne, later invited me to teach there. I taught the subject of Neuromarketing and then Digital Marketing & Consumer Behavior. I had commenced teaching before I had even graduated. I wasn't always an underperforming student, when I went back to university the second time I had a lot more confidence, started to 'feel normal' and ended up top of the class for the neuromarketing subject. I then went on to work for Neuro-Insight who really were the pioneers in applying neuroscience to marketing.

It was at my time with Neuro-Insight that I learned a lot about the field which interested me so much - combining science with marketing, basically applied human behavior. I had never seen anything like neuromarketing until coming across it at the University and during my time working for Neuro-Insight. This internship not only taught me different applications of science and marketing but also made it much easier for me to get the teaching position at the University.

I cite this as a really important time in my career, because to this point I had never done public speaking before and never really had any presentation experience before. I remember the day of my first class as a teacher, I got to the room about 20 minutes early and tried to calm myself down.

I was freaking out and filled with nerves about what to say? What if I go too quickly? What if they think I am a terrible teacher? My anxiety was back and in a big way. I didn't actually know if I could do this. As in literally get up in front of a classroom and facilitate their learning. And this was only a room of 15-20 students! (Mind you though, to this date I still believe University students are the hardest audience to win over).

Long story short, I was received very well by the students. I think my youth really helped because I was pretty much the same age as them. Regardless this was the beginning of forcing myself to speak and to be an educator. This for me started the confidence and started the ball rolling towards being the speaker I wanted to be.

What I realized was that I could be as frightened and as socially awkward as ever during one on one or small group interactions yet be a completely different person on a stage when the eyes, expectation and pressure were all on me. There's a few reasons for this, let's break them down:

1. Alter Ego.
   If you ever get a chance read Todd Herman's book, Alter Ego. He was also one of my first ever mentors, back when I was still trying to be a pro tennis player, and years later he wrote this phenomenal book called Alter Ego. As a tennis player, I had to get into an Alter Ego state all the time. I was this shy, introverted kid in everyday life, but when you saw me on the court, it was a whole different ball game. You would see a competitive beast, nothing shy about him there. I applied the same principle to speaking. I couldn't be the shy, introvert, socially awkward

guy on stage, I had to play at a higher level and step into my best self.

2. Embarrassment.
   I get embarrassed easily. Speaking & presenting forces me to be in a situation whereby if I do mess up, the embarrassment of me being shy and awkward on stage would be so monumental, that I would have no other option but to deliver a great performance every single time. The situation forces me to perform, in order to avoid the embarrassment of failure and social awkwardness.

3. Judgment, Situational Confidence & Control Of The Environment.
   The last part that plays into this, is that in a small group or one on one setting if the other person judges you and doesn't like you, you can tell. You can tell when someone is getting bored in the conversation or if they are trying to leave the conversation, and that obviously doesn't make you feel good. Well when you have an audience in front of you of 20, 100, 1,000 people guess what, the judgment of the few doesn't even matter because you can't tell! I couldn't care less if 200 people out of 400 don't like me when I'm on stage, because there is no way to tell! When you are the speaker you have control of the environment, everyone's eyes are on you, it's whatever you want to say. Unlike a smaller group conversation where the other person's communication to you, changes how you respond back. There's no guesswork like there is in a one on one situation. So I was able to harness the situational confidence of being the speaker that everyone is waiting for to allow me to present the way I know that I can.

I know that most people are the complete opposite to me. They would much rather have a one on one conversation or small group conversation with friends, than stand in front of 1,000 strangers and deliver a presentation (let alone make an offer to them). Well that's why I mentioned the pain and suffering of not being able to hold small group conversations, this made me that much hungrier and more persistent in mastering the skill that few people ever have, because very few people ever have the need to learn these social skills.

Of course being the speaker in fact made me more friends, because people would now approach me and I already had the authority of being the guy that they just saw on stage for the last two hours, versus the other way around where they have no idea who I am and the pressure is on to make an impression. I completely understand that this is only situational confidence but it's a million times better than no confidence.

From teaching at University to a "Real Job"

Towards the end of my University degree I started my first business, named EJD Media. Primarily it started off focusing on helping small businesses with SEO, search engine optimisation, basically helping local businesses rank higher on Google. My first client was my personal trainer at the time and I got him to the top of Google, The business then expanded into selling educational courses helping other marketers improve their SEO skills too. However this income wasn't enough to make a living, so much to my parents delight, I got a real job.

It was a job in Sydney, so I had to relocate from Melbourne. But before I did that, I attended a seminar with my mum to see Gary Vaynerchuk speak. I knew that I wanted to have a business that could sustain me. I wanted to learn how to do that and I thought I would learn that here.

Well at the seminar there were about 8 speakers all up. Just before lunchtime this loud and somewhat aggressive Canadian speaker came on stage jumping up and down about how he is the number one business and wealth coach in the world. His name was JT Foxx. He was very different, much more confident than the other speakers and he would cold read members of the audience so effortlessly. He made some big promises, some big claims and showed a lot of celebrities that he has done events with. A couple of hours later I ended up buying his $4,000 program.

At the time I was freaking out, I barely had $4,000 to my name and it was my mum who actually pushed me to get the program, so I gave it a shot. It was for a 2 day event but I couldn't attend the next one, I had to wait until the following year which was when I was to be living in Sydney. This was the first (and I believe only) time that I had bought something from a platform speaker. He was very proficient at it, perhaps the best I had seen in terms of closing ratio and effectiveness. And once again I was introduced and reminded almost 6 years later of the power of platform speaking. Doing the math in my head, it was well over $500,000 in 2 hours that this speaker did that day, it could have even been over 1 million, I lost count there were way too many people. The other speakers had barely any sales in comparison.

So 2018 comes around, I've now relocated to Rhodes, NSW, and am working at Nestlé. Remember, the first reason I even wanted to start an online business was so that I wouldn't have to go and work in a job, because I was so scared of people! Well the first business wasn't making enough money for me to do that yet so I had to get a job.

Nestle hired me to help them get started and launched on Amazon in Australia because of my online marketing background. Now when I accepted the position, I was of the belief that it would help me gain more skills and knowledge because surely a company as big as Nestlé had to have some really professional experienced digital marketers that I can learn from. To my surprise that was not the case. In fact, not only was that not the case, I was expected to be the only person working on the Amazon project and I was expected to have the most knowledge out of anyone in the company (on an entry level wage mind you, and living expenses in Sydney aren't exactly cheap). Literally no one knew anything about marketing on Amazon, listing on Amazon or anything to do with Amazon.

What surprised me even more was that the ecommerce team really didn't have any ecommerce skills. They didn't implement anything, they outsourced the ecommerce and then reported on it. Only one person actually knew how to run a Facebook ad, everyone else I honestly have no idea what they were doing. This is not a slight on anyone, but it was a wake up call that none of these big businesses have implementers, they are for the most part talking heads who love to do 101 meetings per week. This was a serious flaw in the company, even their own digital marketing team wasn't really a digital marketing team, they had literally zero clue about running ads online, zero. I didn't learn anything about what I wanted to learn, which was advertising online.

Although I didn't get what I wanted from the job itself, Sydney was transformational for me and probably where I believe I got my 'start'. Not only was the personal growth immense, it was the first time I ever lived on my own. The environment put me on the path I needed to focus on actually building a business. Everyday after work had finished I would work on either acquiring new clients or learning new skills to continue getting results for clients. I also made a couple of friends whilst at Nestle, and one in particular, Alex, also helped me with some sales and cold calling. What I did know for sure was that my skill set far exceeded the skill set of the people above me in Nestlé's ecommerce and digital marketing team, I deserved to earn more and have more success.

The timing of everything that happened within my 6 months stint in Sydney was almost perfectly timed to force me to where I am today. I don't believe in a lot of that 'manifestation' or divine interference chatter, but if there was any time where it may have occurred it would be during this time period…

When I got to Nestlé, my first boss, Michael, was fantastic. In fact if he stayed there I don't even know if I would have left Nestlé, I may even still be working there today. I do believe that in business and in a career you have people you want to work for or work with, Michael was one of those people.

Very approachable, understanding and measured in everything that needed to be done. Despite my extreme social awkwardness STILL, (this was 2018 I was 23 years old), he did his best to make me feel comfortable in the new environment.

However, maybe 2 or 3 months into me starting, he announced he was leaving to go and take up an offer as Managing Director of Faber-Castell. At first I was really not happy that this was happening, however looking back it was the best thing that could have happened because it instigated me wanting to leave Nestlé too. The new boss came in, and let's just say I wasn't exactly fond of the change. As soon as my contract ended I left. Leading up to the final weeks of my role there, I still wasn't sure if this was the right move, I had nothing else lined up and my business wasn't ready to completely replace my income. However the day before I was supposed to leave Nestlé my mum told me that my grandmother had passed away unexpectedly. If that wasn't a clear enough sign that I needed to go back home, I don't know what was.

Whilst working in the bureaucratic red tape of an organization as large as this, there were key moments that I did outside of work that helped to launch my business. Firstly, the 2 day event I paid $4,000 for was in Sydney in February, just a few weeks after I started my role. This two day event blew my mind about what was possible in business and once again I found myself paying for the next offer. I paid $8,000 for a four day event called Dream Team that was taking place in July. I also bought into a membership to join a networking group that caught up most weeks with other business owners, most of them much more established than I was.

Even to attend the 2 day event I was freaking out and was extremely nervous about talking to other people. I was close to not going and tried to find every excuse to avoid attending. In fact I don't really think I spoke to anyone during this 2 day event. It was also ambitious of me to sign up for a networking group when that is probably the least desirable activity for someone like me to do! But I was in Sydney, on my own, may as well try it out.

Although the 2 day event didn't get my business off the ground, it was never supposed to. It got the ball rolling, and I was focused to get ready for the July Dream Team Event. Before that though, to my great appreciation, I was able to rope in my friend Alex to come with me to the networking group meetup. I personally don't think I could or would have gone on my own. I don't really talk to anyone, but Alex is great at talking so he naturally finds someone to talk to and gets into a conversation, two or three minutes later he is introducing me and the person he is talking to wants to have a chat with me about me doing their marketing for them. Out of nowhere I had a solid lead thanks to Alex.

The lady's name was Ruth, and we would go on to be friends and work with each other for a while. She was kind of a middle man between an organization and a speaker. A platform speaker. He happened to live in Singapore, but he was coming to Sydney for his upcoming events that she wanted me to market. And so it began, my introduction to working for a platform speaker in the industry I eventually wanted to get into myself.

The marketing went great, the room was packed, he made his sale, everyone happy. Ruth introduced me to this speaker, his name was Resh. To this day Resh and I are still friends. We both instantly connected, probably because we were a similar age and on the same kind of path. He was much further along his path than I was, but nonetheless I knew that these were the sorts of people I needed to be around.

Resh was an incredible platform speaker, he even got invited to speak at events where Grant Cardone and Gary Vaynerchuk were the main speakers. He knew what he was doing and he was a pro. We spent some time hanging out and strategising for future events and plans as well, they didn't quite eventuate but we stayed in contact. I knew that this was the industry I wanted to be in.

Then July comes, it's Dream Team. Do I attend, do I not attend? I barely got the go ahead to take leave from my job for a few days thankfully. Mind you, I only have about 6 weeks left on my contract. Dream Team was the extension of the 2 day event that I bought from JT Foxx. He is a polarizing figure, I won't get into the ins and outs of it but I don't think he is my biggest fan anymore. Regardless he is probably the best closer I have seen and he has a very direct style of communication which can alienate people. For me I enjoy that direct, no bullshit approach.

Well at Dream Team, it was not JT, it was his coaches. To his credit, his coaches are phenomenal. Most coaching companies do not have great coaches, they give you the B team or the C team instead of the person you buy from and it is a real let down. This was not the case at Dream Team.

We had four coaches and all of them brought something different to the table. The four coaches were Cherie, Les, Reggie & Kevin. These individuals would end up becoming quite important throughout my story. I was one out of maybe 100 participants, I think the youngest, definitely the quietest, I was terrified and excited at the same time. To this day I think it was the best event I have ever been to. The people, the atmosphere, the transformation I had was something I have never experienced anywhere else. It wasn't one of those events where they just pump you full of good emotions and high five the person next to you and all the dancing, I can't stand that. This event was full of information. In this kind of environment the coaches are basically seen as gods and you can only hope to get a bit of their attention. These are people you look up to and try to soak up whatever you can get. I hoped I could get maybe a conversation, I usually am overlooked because I don't speak up, but what I ended up getting was far more than what I think anyone expected.

It was day 2 that I had what they call the 'Hot Seat'. This was when I went from the shy quiet kid in the corner, to someone that everyone was jumping to get to know. The Hot Seat is where you sit in front of the four coaches, you tell them what you do and what you want to do and they give you coaching advice. I basically got a massive wake up call on that Hot Seat and a lot of praise too for the skills that I had and the results I had gotten for the clients so far, but I had to do more of it. The new business name was born, My Million Dollar Funnels, and this was the start of an incredible launch. I met people there that are still friends now like Jerry Farsoun & Patty Duque, if you speak to them they can tell you how shy and awkward I was. I also had about 3 or 4 new clients from that one event. With just 6 weeks before the end of my Nestlé contract, things were starting to fall into place just at the right time.

Day 3 of the event comes around, and wow, Cherie was the first ever speaker to have me crying in public. Literally I was crying in a public setting, I couldn't believe it. It was then that I learned how to speak at an emotional level. Cherie is the kind of speaker I would buy anything from, she may even be the best I have seen. She was the coach that pulled me out of my shell, and I couldn't thank her enough for it. In fact I couldn't even speak to her during the event. I was that anxious and shy, I was intimidated by her (I was pretty much intimidated by anyone back then), but she had a power and confidence that I don't think I had ever seen before.

I owe it to her for getting me out of my shell, I really do. We spoke for like one second on the last day, actually I don't think I got a word out, I just said thank you and hugged her and started crying again. I wish I could have said more, I was so upset with myself, but luckily that wasn't the last time we would see each other. In fact Cherie till this day still has a massive influence on my life, she was the one that wrote the foreword in this book and we are about to do some events together as a duo.

The end of day 3 comes around, and Reggie makes us all an offer. The offer was basically you get one on one coaching plus lifetime access to any future Dream Team events.The price? $33,500. Yeah, there's no typo in that. I barely had enough money to pay rent in Sydney, I just finished university and I already put in $12,000 to get to this event. So I didn't express any interest. I had about $14,000 left in my bank account at the time, which was not enough.

That night though, some of the attendees go for dinner at the hotel and they are telling me I should consider it. The person sitting next to me, a lovely lady named Debbie, tells me that if she were my age she would definitely do it. So they convince me (like dejavu) and I put my name on the list for a conversation.

Day 4 comes around and I have the conversation with Reggie. Reggie also intimidated me at the time, I haven't seen much of him at this stage and I don't know exactly what he is about. They say he used to work with Tony Robbins for 10 years so that was impressive. Anyway this conversation goes for about 45 minutes. I could tell he was getting a bit antsy as he had many people to talk to. I can't believe I found myself literally considering paying $33,500 for further support. My hands were trembling, I barely said many words, until I reached the decision point in my brain and did it. I was able to do a payment plan $8,000 on the day and then $8,500 a month until it was paid off. No I did not ask or tell anyone like my parents, because they probably would have said I am crazy. I still to this day do not think they know I put down $33,500 back then when I didn't have the money (and still had a student debt).

The best decisions you make don't come from playing safe though, and they definitely do not come from asking for permission. There comes a time where you need to back yourself. How did I justify it to myself? Simple, I had already probably secured 3 clients from this Dream Team, totalling $10,000 in revenue, if I just attended 3 or 4 more of these I would make back the $33,500 from clients directly acquired from Dream Team events. Especially considering that the coaches position the dream team lifetime students as the experts to go to. Then I worked out that if I keep making $5,000 a month from my job and $3,000 from my business that I will be able to pay the $8,000 a month until it's done. So the client opportunities, the networking with other students all over Australia and the world and networking with the coaches made it a tough but acceptable decision for me.

The last part was choosing which coach I wanted for my one on one calls. I had 16 calls and I could break them up with any of the coaches but had to elect a main coach to start off with. Now maybe to your surprise I didn't actually go with Cherie. Cherie positioned herself as a property expert for most of the event, and I was not ready for property. She also had about every other person select her as their coach so she may have been too busy. I chose Les. Les positioned himself as a platform speaker trainer and he mentioned that he even made over $1,000,000 in a day from speaking one time. He also gave me the business name idea in the hot seat and said he had speaker clients he could introduce me to immediately (another reason that helped me buy the coaching because if he could introduce me to clients I can make the investment back quickly). And so it began, I was found and My Million Dollar Funnels was born.

Apart from the business growth that happened whilst living in Sydney, this was also the place where I first started to remove the feelings of social anxiety. I did this with another coach named Julien. Julien I had learned from when I was in high school on Youtube and now he was offering transformational coaching services. He asked me to do two tasks that changed my life. The first task he said was to go to Sydney Darling Harbour and speak loudly in public about my favourite movie for 5 minutes.

There was nothing scarier in the world than this task at the time. It took me WEEKS to even muster up the courage to do this. I couldn't do it on my own, so again I ask Alex to come with me and we get it done. It was scary, cringeworthy and all that but you know what, once you do it, you realize that literally no one cares. You get some people looking at you but really no one cares, nothing bad happens, people are too busy minding their own business.

The second task was to do a moving vlog, recording myself on my phone, speaking loudly whilst walking through crowds of people. Again seemingly at first very scary, but then it became like second nature.

Julien forced me to do tasks that scared me like crazy, which made other social interactions seem so much easier to do. This was probably the only thing I consciously did to try to remove the social awkwardness and anxiety. After this, getting on stage and speaking really did not seem so scary because the stage is much more in my control compared to speaking about random topics on my phone to random people passing by.

Sydney was transformational in more ways than one, but my next step: saying goodbye to Sydney, goodbye to Nestlé and committing myself to building this business and becoming a speaker.

3

Momentum

I get back to Melbourne and this is when I realize exactly what I've done. I've burned the boats. The stable income was gone, I had a small but ok income from the business, I have put myself towards a $33,500 commitment with money I didn't yet have and I had no other options now, I had to make this work. The thing is though, whenever I put myself in financially difficult or strenuous positions, it has always forced me to find a way to make even more. It was no different now, I went straight to work with execution and focus that I had not seen in myself since my pursuit of tennis.

Burning the boats so to speak, isn't something many people commit to. I don't necessarily recommend quitting your job or having only one option, unless you're a certain type of person. For me, although I have always had social issues, something I have never wavered in, is my innate belief and confidence in my ability to do things that most people can't and to achieve outcomes that most people won't. I don't exactly know why I have always had this belief, especially considering how scared I was in other areas of my life, but it's always been there. Perhaps because it had to be there, I had to make up somehow for what I so severely lacked socially. Regardless, I would only recommend quitting your job or going all in once your business has replaced your income and/or you are the type of person that makes success happen.

It does sound perhaps narcissistic, however it isn't, and for those who feel the same way about themselves, that you just find a way to make success happen no matter what it is you do and commit to, then you understand completely what I mean.

I first came across the notion of burning the boats, from a film called Into The Wild. The main character Chris has a wealthy family and essentially is sick and tired of material possessions. He goes off into the wilderness to find fulfillment in nature and experience. He burns his cash, his identity and basically any of his possessions that mainstream society deems necessary for success. Instead he leaves his family and sets off into the wild.

Now obviously this isn't that extreme, but it's the same concept. Leaving all else behind you so that you can only have one outcome otherwise you fail. When there is no plan B, you better be sure Plan A is going to work. One of the most important elements to making sure Plan A works is momentum. It's hard to get but once you have it, you need to try to never let it go. Once you lose it, it can take years to get back. So I hit the ground running.

After that dream team event I already had a few clients that came on board, I then started my coaching with Coach Les immediately & I attended more of the Dream Team's as I was now a lifetime member. This allowed me to network with more business owners and become closer to the coaches. It was at my second Dream Team that I met Marcus, another student, and for whatever reason we instantly connected and to this day we still partner with each other on different projects. I also met Tony, Reggie's assistant, and became closer to the coaches Reggie, Cherie & Kevin.

Then a funny thing started to happen. I was finally doing what I thought I wanted, an online business so that I wouldn't have to get a job and therefore not be around people all the time. Well most of that was happening, except

I was talking to more people now than in any of the jobs I had ever had! I didn't even recognise myself. Mostly I credit Jerry for this as he kept inviting me to networking events and strategising together in his offices.

I realized though, anyone can start their own business, anyone can do this, I needed to not lose sight of what I wanted, which was to become a speaker. And why did that motivate me? Because I get motivated by things that the vast majority are either scared of, can't do or won't do. Speaking is definitely one of those things.

It was August when I would get my first shot. The opportunity arose from the networking group I signed up to at the other event. They allowed you to do one ten minute presentation and so I thought let's do it. I had never spoken before, but I so desperately wanted to. I start telling my parents and some of my new business friends about it, I don't even know what I am speaking about at this stage and I ask Les for some advice too. Many were asking if I was getting paid to speak. I thought, what, paid? Why would I be getting paid?

See, many people even to this day think I am motivated by money. That is completely wrong, if you think that, you simply don't know me. I couldn't care less about getting paid for a speaking gig. I just wanted to get up on the stage and do something interesting.

I am motivated by setting an example to others. Originally I was motivated by making myself interesting and to stand out because that is when I would have the most opportunities for interactions and make more connections. It meant I made faster connections because people came up to me, and it allowed me to reduce my social anxiety because others started the conversation with me. I was also able to start desensitizing myself to speaking to large audiences.

In fact I am desensitized to the value of money itself. I don't recommend being like that necessarily, but to me I don't think of money as an essential. Money can't give you shelter, you cannot eat it and you cannot drink it, it is how you use money that gets you to where you want to go. People place way too high a value on money and that's when they get emotional and off balance. If you're motivated purely by making more money, it will be a never ending painful battle of always wanting more of it. When you do something valuable and worthwhile, make a name for yourself, then money will follow and it will be nice and you will be able to do more things of course, but for me money is not the main driver. In fact I turn down many opportunities to get more money, it doesn't do it for me.

One time someone asked me "if you make so much in your business why do you still have to teach at the University of Melbourne?" I'm just there saying "have to? Who said anything about having to?" I teach at the University because I enjoy it, because that's me giving back to the students who actually want to be taught by someone with practical skills and who has built a business, rather than those only quoting theory and literature. That's me giving back because when I was a student I would have LOVED to have a teacher who actually could walk the walk instead of just reading from a textbook. That's why I do it, why does everything have to be about money?

I also have worked at the Australian Open every year for the last 10 years, on about $25 an hour for a whole month which means I can't work on my business. If I was driven by money, to put it simply, I would be acting quite differently. You need to find deeper drivers than money, because when you come up against an opponent who is motivated by something with intangible drive, you will lose almost every time. It's like the tennis player or basketball player who is happy to just 'compete' and win a few games so they get paid, but they don't love it or have a desire to win a championship.

You think Roger Federer is primarily driven by money? Rafael Nadal? Michael Jordan? Kobe Bryant. Hell no. I'm not saying it isn't part of it or maybe wasn't at the beginning, but you don't get to the top of your field being primarily motivated by money. They are motivated by winning, by legacy, by beating their best version of themselves. Once your body starts giving in, your mind starts faltering, you think money is going to get you over the line? Not a chance. Good luck if that's your sole driver, you'll need it.

Regardless, I digress. August comes along and it is the time of the event. I am so nervous. Social anxiety plus general anxiety disorder, when waiting in a room with an audience there and I am about to speak to them, I don't know who any of them are, except Jerry and I don't even know how this speech is going to sound, let's just say it's a formula for extreme anxiety to show itself in the moment. I am as quiet as a mouse usually so anyone that did know me was not expecting anything amazing to happen, let's just say that. I don't mind that because if the expectation is so low, the only way you can really go is up right? Well it's time, my name is called…

I get up to the area of where the speakers stand and they hand me this weird looking device. I'm standing there waiting for them to do something with it, and then I realize, oh this is the microphone… and I need to plug it on myself, oh and it's already on? Ah shit.

So I'm standing at the front of the room and trying to get this mic to go on properly, and I really had no idea what I was doing, so at this point anyone that didn't know me surely has to also have their expectations set to super low as well. The mic drops to the floor, and the massive cord is just hanging down from my shirt. It is very awkward, all of these background and static noises are coming from the mic, I can hear some of the crowd starting to laugh, and then finally someone comes to help me. Ahh what a start.

Anyway, it's game time, alter ego time, show's on, let's go. And 'go' I did. There is nowhere to hide when you are the one with the mic, nowhere to run, nowhere to shy away from what is going on. Ethan could no longer be with us during the presentation, he would have tried to hide, perhaps he would have stood to the corner of the stage and speak in a low, muffled voice hoping no one would judge or hear the words coming out of his mouth, walking on eggshells hoping not to offend anyone or say the wrong thing or something that people would disagree with. Nope, this has to be the competitor in me coming out.

I took up the center of the stage and delivered, I don't even know what I said, all I remember is how it felt. And it felt powerful. Everyone in the room was in shock and awe, like what the heck, those words at that volume just came out of his mouth? No way. It's crazy my whole voice projection and demeanor completely change to this confident guy when I jump on stage.

I walked off to a great applause, and just about everyone there (even the headline speaker) asked for my business card that I actually ran out of them. Then at the end people were even asking for my photo! I had no idea what was going on. But I did know one thing though, let's do it again.

I posted about the event on Facebook, and some of the attendees commented about how much they enjoyed it. My first time ever and the feedback was amazing, I couldn't be happier.

Although this is when I experienced tall poppy syndrome. Tall poppy syndrome, unfortunately when you start behaving and achieving things that most people won't get to, you'll have some haters trying to pull you down. The most prevalent hater or disbeliever? Someone that has known you for a while and has come to 'expect' a certain behavior from you. This could be your parents, a partner, a sibling, a close friend.

I couldn't believe my ears when someone who had known me from year 10, who was supposed to be a coach, a mentor, someone who I could trust, told me 'oh what would they know they just said that you did well to make you feel good.' I was like what the heck. This person has known me from my shyest, most uncomfortable self, and he would have darn well known how hard it would have been for me to get up on stage and do that regardless if it was good, shit or somewhere in between and he still said that?

There comes a time where you have to cut out the people that have an old version of you stored in their memory that they won't let you outgrow. Those that think you should behave or act in the way you have always behaved and acted, which obviously by definition gives you no room to grow. They want you stagnant, to keep themselves comfortable so that they don't need to push themselves to grow too. It makes them feel bad about themselves if you grow, how ironic. You can't keep these people in your life, you simply can't. You also can't allow it to derail you. For me this was big, this was someone I really trusted, it made me think about his comments for a while and doubt myself for ages.

Now when writing this I have received heaps of that kind of rubbish from random people and it doesn't even register any more. The response in my head is 'whatever, you have no idea what you are talking about', but if you haven't experienced this kind of behavior or response before, the first time can shake you. It makes a lot of people quit before they even get started, remember the issue is with the person that said it, they are hurting and have things they need to address about themselves, the issue is not with you. In fact once you start getting those kinds of haters and disbelievers, it means you are doing a good job.

After this event I'm constantly looking for more opportunities. There is a powerful part of the brain you should know about called your reticular activating system (RAS), essentially your RAS helps you to focus on what it is you are actively seeking, you're essentially brainwashing your brain to always be on the lookout for what you want. For me this was more opportunities.

One came around thanks to Reggie. Reggie worked for JT Foxx, and essentially he gave me a couple of chances to give an on stage testimonial at some of the events. There was one massive event coming up in October where JT was speaking at the same event as Gary Vaynerchuk, yes the Gary V that I had gone to see speak a year ago before any of this had started for me. Janine Allis was also a guest speaker here. JT's team had asked me to give a testimonial at this event, wow what a shift from a year ago. To JT's credit he is a big branding guy, so anytime his students are on stage even for things like this, he allows them to take photos. So not only was I about to get on stage in front of a few thousand people in my hometown just one year since I was an attendee here, but I was going to get photos of myself in front of a thousand people. That is a massive branding opportunity.

I get there, and I see the size of that crowd and again I am like oh shit what have I gotten myself into? We go backstage, we walk past the massive audience, at least 2-3,000 people were there, I'm too nervous to even take it all in, but I am essentially seeing behind the scenes of what goes into a massive event like this (which believe it or not just 2.5 years after this I would go on to produce my own, more on that later). I get the mic, the guys behind me get some crazy good photos, everyone's happy and just like that it's over. What a rush. I used that photo for ages on my website. I just knew that I wanted that rush again and again. Here it was, the first sign of the speaker's addiction.

Some questioned my focus and asked why don't you just focus on client acquisition, as these gigs aren't paying the bills yet. And to that I reply I'm playing a longer term game. Yes I could have probably gotten more paying clients instead of focusing on getting on stages, but I knew long term, my best self and my most successful self was by being on stage.

Most people can't think a month ahead, let alone a year. Whether it's in business, relationships, health - whatever it is, most fall into their old patterns of thinking, their old logic and their flawed sense of safety in the past which means they never strategise for the future. No one could see my dream outcome except me, no one could fathom I would be a speaker but me, if there was a title for least likely to be a speaker it would have been me. Well here I was, coming fast up the ranks, good luck trying to stop it.

After this was done, there were about 4 weeks until I was going on a 45 day holiday to Europe. The thing was though, I was so hooked on this new found sense of confidence and ability that I really didn't want my momentum to go away because of a holiday. So once again I got creative and started asking around. I thought to myself, hang on, if I can get a gig speaking overseas, by definition I become an 'international speaker'. I text my coach Les, mind you this is about 2 weeks now before I am set to fly, I had no hope I thought. But less than 2 days later, he comes back and says, "You're going to Switzerland right?" I say "yes". He says meet Valeria & Cedric. I speak to them a bit, they say they have an event on November 22nd and they need a speaker. I arrive on November 19th, so that is perfect. And just like that, I have a speaking gig booked for Zurich, Switzerland. What a world.

We get closer to the event and they say that the date of the event has changed, it is now on November 19th. So that means I arrive at 9am and speak at about 7pm. Which normally I guess that's ok, but this is a 24 hour transit period from Melbourne to Zurich, I am going to be extremely jetlagged, and I can't sleep on planes! Here's what you do though, you say yes, and you figure out the rest. I will always find a way to do everything that I want. They also tell me, you're the main speaker now. So instead of a 10 minute slot, you have 30 minutes.

Now I'm freaking out, I have less than 2 weeks to make a 30 minute presentation. I have never spoken for this long, what if I finish too early? I'm the main speaker, but I have never been a headline speaker before, I don't even have a presentation yet! What if they don't understand my accent, is this all moving too fast? Ahh self doubt, a killer of many dreams. I had these thoughts for all of 5 seconds then got on with the job. This is what I'm doing, this is who I am now, this is exactly where I want and need to be. I might not be 'ready' but who the hell ever is ready, and why do so many people feel the need to wait to be ready in the first place? Start before you are ready as

Reggie always said.

Give me the stage, the lights, the audience and I will perform. Jet lagged, middle of the night, no presentation, no fancy clothes, different country, don't speak the language, never spoken for this long before, no worries. You can make all the excuses you want, I just choose to execute and let someone else worry about them. Yes I was extremely tired, but the crowd couldn't tell. I gave it everything and absolutely smashed it. This was the first time I had a glimpse of what stardom felt like.

At the end of my presentation there was a line, yes a line of people waiting to take a photo with me, shake my hand and tell me how much they enjoyed it. I couldn't believe it, this shy introverted kid who couldn't speak to his family or friends was on the other side of the world, where they speak another language and the audience was lining up to take photos with him. I didn't think it was real.

Sure the attention and accolades were amazing especially for someone like me who had really never experienced anything like it before, but you know what else was happening, I was talking to more people, meeting more people, making friends and connections all over the world. Even today people who were at that seminar still ask me, when are you coming back to Switzerland? I was not only becoming a good speaker and business owner but I was conquering my biggest weakness at the same time and even turning it into my biggest strength. At just 24 years old this was more than I ever dreamed was possible. And yet I wanted more, and knew I was capable of more, admittedly though even I didn't expect the extreme growth that happened from here over the next two and a bit years.

It can be the same for you, you don't even know what you're capable of yet, sometimes you just need someone to believe in you before you can even believe in yourself. Sometimes you just need to close your eyes and move in the direction of what you want, turn off that thinking brain and you'll see what happens.

How would your behavior change if you knew that anything you did would turn out successful? What would you do differently if someone told you that you were going to achieve your dream outcome if you just stayed the path? I challenge you to do that.

How much quicker would you move, how much more confidence would you have behind every move that you made and how much more sure of yourself would you feel? Maybe you would stop asking disempowering questions or caving into those disempowering thoughts, and instead you'd have some certainty and conviction behind what you were doing.

4

Unstoppable Acceleration : The Student Begins Ascension

I thought it couldn't get any better than 2018. Have you ever felt that way? That what you have done was so unbelievable that surely it couldn't get any better from here, that there was nowhere else to go? For me it's quite a common false thought pattern, luckily it is just that, false. Boy was I wrong, 2019 was a whole new level that I could never have anticipated.

In 2018, all of my speaking opportunities were on someone else's stage, they were keynote events. They weren't my events, I was just invited to go and speak at them. It was like getting my training wheels so to speak. Well 2019 was when magic happened and my dream of running my own events came true.

It started with another dream team event, where Reggie threw out the idea of me, him and Tony running events together. Like I said I always say yes to any opportunity, and figure out the rest later. Reggie was a pro, he had been doing this for ages, working with Tony Robbins and then JT, this is the guy I needed to learn from and what better way than to be on the road with him, learning in real time. This was the guy who initially sold me on the $33,500 coaching program, and someone I used to find intimidating. Although I still wasn't fully comfortable socially around him or really anyone still, I forced myself to figure it out as I went along. It was surreal.

So the decision was made and it was time to create the plan. Where would we do our first event? He lived in California, USA and I lived in Melbourne, Australia. He wasn't too keen on doing too much flying because he spent so much of his year in planes, and for me well I was more than keen to fly and get exposed to the speaker world, so closer to Reggie it was.

Let's not underestimate the impact Reggie had on my life. I don't think that I would get to where I am today or even past this point in this book if it weren't for Reggie. The reason being is that without his push and belief in me I really don't know how I would have got started with my own events. I had no plans on my own to randomly pick a city and run an event, it was him that poked the bear. It was him that believed in me before I even believed in myself. This was someone I felt like I couldn't let down, and with most things I valued other people more than I valued myself.

Even when I was playing tennis I would always perform better in team events instead of solo events, because I was playing for other people, they relied on me. It took awhile for me to realize I could value myself like that too. So once Reggie threw the idea out there I knew the opportunity wasn't going to be there long and I valued his support and opinion too much to let him down. I had known him even whilst I was in Nestle still, he would do coaching calls with me and was a huge help to even get out of my job in the first place. I had to make the most out of this and make it work.

He decided on Colorado Springs. Somewhere I had never heard of before, a smaller city in Colorado. He had family there and the idea was also to test it out first with a smaller event to test the model. So Colorado it was and we were going in May. Just like in a movie, I felt like the plan was set and we were about to launch into something amazing.

My biggest concern though, was what if the event failed and he didn't want to do anymore with me? Most people would be concerned with the expenses involved, I really didn't care, not because I had so much money, I actually didn't, remember this is still early days in my business, but because I knew the long game would be much better for me with Reggie in it. I had never sold from the stage before, and now I went from a 30 minute presentation to what was now a whole 6-8 hour event, with my name on the room. Reggie was to speak for two hours and I would speak for the rest. I needed to create content, and fast.

For this, I went back to Cherie. Cherie and I always had a strong relationship since we talked a few times during different Dream Team events. Here she selflessly coached me on my first presentation to close. She asked me to create a quick 30 minute presentation that I could perform for her and then she would critique it. We did this a few times and I finally started to understand how to not only create a presentation but how to close from stage (details to come later).

Most speakers have the luxury (or maybe it's the opposite) of only needing to speak. For me, I also had to fill the rooms, yes get the actual audience to the event. Just because we set an event date and location, didn't mean people were going to show up or even knew about the event. My job was to do what I do, which is run ads to fill the event, Reggie's job was to find the location and handle the hotel and travel arrangements.

We thought a smaller city would mean less competition and therefore lower cost per registration for the ads. Well that was wrong. The reality is, if the area isn't accustomed to attending events like this, it takes more convincing and actually a higher cost per lead because there are less people to market to. It took about 36 hours from when the ads went live to the time the first person signed up for the event. When that first person came through I was super pumped, wow someone wanted to actually see me speak! There was no one else on the ads or the marketing. I was finally doing it! We ultimately had 160 people sign up for the event. Not as many as I wanted, but I didn't care. It was the first time and that's quite a lot of people who wanted to see me, a complete stranger coming to their city.

It's May. It's time to get to the airport. Now we have our next obstacle, I'm not great with flying. And by not great, I mean extremely anxious. I have certain airlines I like and certain types of planes I like but generally speaking I can get very nervous, again another anxiety trait that stems from my generalized anxiety disorder. I reluctantly got to the airport, and tried to mentally prepare myself for 24 hours in transit. But my mind wandered. It wasn't just 24 hours there, it was the fact it was 3 flights, 3 take offs, 3 landings, an uber to the hotel and then I had to do it all again to go back home just a few days later. This is compounded by how my brain works… I ruminate over these types of thoughts for a while to the point of intoxication.

When I was training to be a tennis player I always knew traveling was part of the package, and I was ok with it. I figured if I could be a pro tennis player I would get over my fear of flying. Well speaking is essentially the same if not more traveling when you do it properly. So I guess here I was, finding the next best thing to tennis and in fact almost copying the exact lifestyle of a professional tennis player anyway.

I'm at the airport, I check in and go to the gate. Then this wave hits me. Is it really worth it? What if no one comes to the event? Why am I even wasting my time, this is silly. And for the first time since I was a young kid, I burst out in tears in public. I'm literally just sitting there at the airport, crying alone, trying to keep silent so no one notices. And here it was, the first sign of it. The famous success ceiling. I wasn't crying because I was scared of flying, I had been on many flights before all over the world, I had never cried about it. Yes it was my first time going alone overseas but I was going to meet Reggie on the other side. I was $10,000 USD in for this event, and I couldn't care less, I wanted to get out of the airport and go back home, I didn't care about the money. This fear though was nothing to do with flying, this was my success ceiling, and if you're not careful yours will sabotage your dreams.

You will have different success ceilings that come up for you during your path to your dream result. If you don't, it means you are not pushing yourself. A success ceiling shows itself when you are about to make a giant leap between your old self and your desired new self. Our brains are lazy, they want us to stay comfortable, they don't care if we thrive and become our best version of ourselves. We are wired to just get by and do the bare minimum to survive. That's it. The success ceiling is your brain shouting at you 'Hang on we don't know what lies here, this is dangerous, this is new, and there is no going back from this.' It can show itself in many ways - anger, frustration, emotions. For me this one was coming up in a lot of sadness, fear and crying. Strong negative emotions as I was making the shift between my old self and my ideal self. It can seem easy to throw it in and give up when this happens.

The issue that most people make is that once they get here they revert back to old habits and never break through the ceiling. They ask their old friends, their family, whatever is 'safe' in their brain. Why? Because your brain knows what they will say. For example if I was in that airport and texted my mum she may have said "it's ok darling, we can come pick you up, there's no need to go if you are feeling like this." And that comes from a place of love and support but it doesn't help breakthrough to the next level, and you damn well know that if you talk to certain people they are going to reaffirm your comfortable little brain's ideologies of staying the same and not progressing to the next level.

You need to shut off the thinking mind and proceed towards what is causing the pain. This is extremely important, whatever causes you pain and the feeling of being uncomfortable that's what you need to seek, not avoid. That's where the growth happens. Stop asking your old network, your average high school friends, your family that doesn't necessarily see your drive for personal development. Stop relying on what has made you comfortable in the past. I had to get on that bloody plane.

I texted coach Les just before boarding. He successfully calmed me down and sent some really touching messages that allowed me to put aside my selfish emotions quite frankly, and get on with the show. He told me that most people would do anything to change places for the opportunity I was about to embark on, and that it's time to step into it. And he was 100% right. I also had Reggie waiting on the other side, he knew I was nervous too and told me to get the Wi-Fi in the plane, if I get scared just message him. Having role models like them, people who had walked the walk, was powerful, these were people I looked up to and I could not let them down. They were playing at a level above me, hence why I relied on them, instead of someone that knew the former me and had expectations of what I should be or how I should act based on my previous suboptimal self. You need to do the same, and if you don't have someone like that, you need to rely on yourself to make the correct decision and blast through each and every success ceiling, which is what I had to do with the Nestlé situation earlier.

You bet I got on that plane. Finally I landed in Los Angeles. I had missed coming to LA, this is one of my favorite places to go. After 16 hours on the plane it is a massive relief to get here. Next flight from LA to Denver, we fly over the Colorado mountains. I am in great spirits now even talking to random people on the plane. I get to Denver and have a bit of time before the third and final flight. This one was the one I dreaded the most. Reggie was meeting me in Denver and we were going on this flight together, so that made me feel better. But I was texting him asking if I could just get an Uber from Denver to Colorado Springs. It was only a bit over an hour drive, but he wanted to get the plane instead. So I waited for him.

Here in Colorado there were strong tornadoes this week and the weather was a bit all over the place, so via car or via plane I guess there were different risks. It gets to the flight, and it is the tiniest plane I have seen in my life. Oh my god it may have fit maybe 50 people max. I knew we were in for a bumpy ride, but I didn't know how bumpy. The flight took off and you could feel every wind gust from the get go, it was insane. The most turbulent flight I had ever been on, the longest 20 minutes of my life, but we landed safely and here I was in Colorado Springs. How happy I am to be here.

This insight should give you confidence. Here I am with more 'silly' nervous worries and anxiety than most people, I get anxious about almost every single thing, I think about all the possibilities and worry about which one may happen and I'm still here doing all these things. If I can do it, anyone reading can.

Colorado Springs is a beautiful, serene place, mountains everywhere, small town and picturesque. I didn't realize that it was a higher altitude so my lips were breaking and cracking over the next few days, and I really could feel the difference of being at this altitude even in my breathing.

We get to the hotel and I am extremely excited, we check out the venue and make sure the room is ready for the event, and then it's into the hotel room finalizing the presentation. Cherie gives me some pointers and last minute advice and then I'm ready to go! We had a few days to get acclimated first, and I recommend this for all events that you are traveling to if you are the main speaker. I do like the hotel lifestyle, I'm not sure if many people do, I think most I meet say the opposite, but for me there's nothing better than a new environment and a focused place on the road for a few days. We go out, enjoy the city and everything feels great.

Spoke too soon…

It's late May, a week before the US summer. It's supposed to be good weather. Well this is Colorado. Anything can happen apparently. The night before the event, there is a blizzard. I've never experienced snow in a city before, we just don't have this in Australia. Don't get me wrong it was beautiful, like really incredible. However, the event is the next day, how are people going to show up if the city is snowed in?

Long story short, the event day is here, and we are getting texts left, right and center from people sending us photos of their car being snowed under, or that the road is closed, and so on and so forth. The snowstorm has made it nearly impossible to get to the event. Out of 160 people, we barely had 15 attend. Show must go on though. Needless to say we had pretty much no sales and the event, revenue wise it was a complete disaster. Yes, I really went through all that just to fail. Back on the plane, back on the 24 hour transit routine to go back home with my tail between my legs and head down.

You see, this is where most people give up. $10,000 USD, complete loss, all that time, money and effort expended for what, nothing? Well, you've got to earn your stripes somehow, I guess this was my moment, what was I going to do from here?

By doing this event, the first one with my name behind it, I learned some invaluable lessons. Don't go to a snowstorm prone area being the first one. I learned that I was actually still not a good speaker in terms of closing. I didn't really have an idea on how to close. I had to fix that. Not once did the question 'should I keep doing this?' actually enter my mind. It was never a question, I knew I had to keep going, I knew I would figure it out.

I can't believe how many people just quit. They have one bad try, 3 bad tries, even ten bad attempts and they just give up and call it quits. My perseverance and persistence has always been there, I am extremely stubborn. The speaking world wasn't going to beat me, I was going to take it. I would do whatever it took to make this work.

5

From Failure to Winning

This time I got on the front foot, I was worried maybe Reggie wouldn't be keen to try again after the first disaster, but he was fine. I suggested we go to Singapore. All of my best results so far were actually clients from Singapore. I have my best friend that lives there, it's a bigger city and a city that loves personal development, business growth and these types of events. Reggie said he had never had a bad event in Singapore. That settles it. We plan to go to Singapore in July. Reggie suggested seeing as we are flying that far, we should add other cities, so we add Malaysia. This time the ads do much better, about 300 on the list for Singapore and 500 for Malaysia. The costs are also much cheaper.

I spent all my time dramatically changing my entire presentation. Now it was built to close, I just knew this would work. I didn't care if there were 5 people or 50 people, I would sell, I was sure of it. Time to close. Time to win.

Back on the plane, arriving in Singapore, staying at the beautiful Shangri-La. Could I afford it? Who knows, but one thing that Les told me was that if you want to perform like a rockstar you better treat yourself like one too. That meant better accommodation. Which drove me even more, I wanted to always stay in places like this, which meant I had to win and I had to perform.

The day arrives and it is a slow start, only 20 people come in and it's almost time to begin the event. Reggie comes over and asks what is going on, why are so few people here? Seems to be a Singapore thing, 10 minutes later the room is packed with about 80 people. It's game time.

This venue also has a stage which is the first time I am on an elevated platform to speak. It felt real. And real it was. I fell in love with Singapore. In fact during 2019 I was in Singapore 6 times. This event was a hit, a big hit and I finally felt what it was like to win as a speaker. To close as a speaker and do it with ease. To be fair, it wasn't even my best. It didn't feel natural yet, I did have moments where I ran out of breath, didn't know what to say or had trouble with energy levels. Regardless, it worked and the show goes on.

Malaysia was next. It is a completely different feel to Singapore. It's not as affluent, but the people in Malaysia made me realize why I was doing this. This was truly a life changing event. Not because of sales, sales were better in Singapore, but because of the people I met here. They were so genuinely inspired and captivated, they made me feel like I was their role model already. They wouldn't let me go, I was there until about 8pm talking, answering questions, taking photos, what a rush. Reggie had to leave earlier so I was all alone, nervous about being in this city on my own, but that all went away with the amazing response from the audience.

I remember going back on the plane home and thinking, 'yeh, if this is what being a speaker is like, I'll figure out my plane anxiety, I will keep working to the bone and I don't care how exhausted I get, this is unlike anything else, unlike any dream, this was reality.' Yes the sales were great and it justified all of my actions that I took to pursue this relentlessly, but it was nothing compared to the rush. I wanted that again. Having that sort of impact on people that just met me is something I never imagined, I now took it as my responsibility. What's next? I asked.

Well I wanted to go back of course and schedule the next events. I was almost on an international flight every week or two at one point. I was racking up those frequent flyer points. Any fear, any anxiety can be turned into your superpower. Remember that.

I get on the plane home, filled with this inspiration and motivation to keep serving people like this. I pull out my phone and I write a list of a tour I want to do, when I can afford it and when the risk justifies the reward. I still have that list with me. I wanted to hold events in ten countries over 4 weeks. The list reads: London, Paris, Amsterdam, Oslo, Helsinki, Stockholm, Estonia, Zurich, Munich then from there over to Canada. At that moment though it wasn't feasible, I had to take one step at a time.

So here is what I did. I planned more events with Reggie: Los Angeles & San Diego. But I also reached out to Les and got him to do some events with me too! We did a whole different style of event called Rockstar Speaker. We moved quickly, we booked in for Singapore & Malaysia in August. So I was to fly home, fly back to Asia, fly back home, fly over to LA and then back home again. A few months ago I would have found this intimidating, now I was feeling like this was me. How many people would be crazy enough to do this? I thought. Very little. I knew that the opportunity and situation I willed myself into was one that the vast majority will never get to experience, and I never took that for granted.

Rockstar Speaker comes around, and Rockstar Speaker is a completely different event. With Reggie the events I do are with me as the main focus, Reggie introduces me and then makes an offer at the end. But the content is me and the sale is about me doing their marketing for those that buy. The idea with Rockstar Speaker was to help me move away from the done for you model, and move more into the education model. Les was really the main speaker although we spoke for an equal amount of time, but he was the one teaching the speaking principles. I would fill up the rooms, he would be the main guy and we were to work like that. He already made $1m in a day as a speaker so I trusted he would be able to close.

However when it came time to do so, I was the one who was to give the pitch in Singapore, and it did not go well. Yes we made some sales, but it wasn't a thunderous success like my first time in Singapore. The offer was not clear. This time the audience was even bigger than the first, we didn't have enough seats in the room and there was a massive line waiting to get in. That's how well the marketing worked. The number of people was not the problem, the offer was. We went to Malaysia, tweaked it a bit, he gave the call to action, we improved a little bit but still not much success. It was not a great start to the Rockstar Speaker events sales wise. Marketing wise though it worked. Boy did it work, we had a line of people waiting to enter, it was packed. In Malaysia it was like a mini stadium with 300+ people fitting into this one room. If you can get the marketing to work, the sales actually are the easier part. So we planned for three events in Australia in October with a whole new offer and close.

I got home from this tour, and I remember being exhausted during this one. Even someone came up to me and said you look tired, are you sure you're going to be up to speak? Make no mistake though, once I got on stage they were like "woah ok then, who are you!?" These two events I think were my best performances speaking wise. I was really starting to come into my own as a speaker and I could command an audience easily now.

I wanted to get some tests done before I set sail for LA in a couple of weeks. The tests showed that I had glandular fever. Not just that I have it but it's likely that I have had it for the last 6 months. No wonder I have been exhausted. How the heck did I even pull this off whilst having glandular fever. In today's world I probably wouldn't have been allowed to leave my house, but for me I didn't care about having this issue, I didn't have major symptoms and clearly I have been dealing with it just fine the last couple of months on the road anyway. Show must go on, and go on it did.

I went over to California for the events with Reggie, another great success, and then I went back home for my first three events on home soil. Rockstar Speaker was revamped, I had adjusted the close, gave it to Les and he performed it.

Before that though I had secured myself an incredible opportunity, a TEDx talk. You've probably heard of TED talks before, it is essentially the pinnacle for any speaker to be able to do a TED talk. I saw the opportunity, the opening, and took it with both hands. It fit perfectly in the calendar, September. The issue was I had no idea what to talk about or how to structure it. It was 16 minutes max and obviously you don't sell anything so it was a whole new format. You also have to stay in a red dot so I cannot move in and out of the audience like I am used to, which by the way helps reduce the anxiety of speaking. Les was a massive help with this talk, he restructured it and optimized it to where it made sense for me. Usually I don't script my talks and I don't recommend doing that either, but here TEDx was different. You needed to know what you were going to say because there was a time limit and also slides that you couldn't just skip over.

This was actually the most nervous I had been for any talk. Funny that. No money on the line, no traveling to do, a tiny audience compared to what I had been used to and no pressure to sell anything! Yet I was a nervous wreck. I listened to my speech before giving it just to make sure I didn't miss any parts. I felt nervous but those in the audience said they enjoyed it and it got quite good feedback. It is on Youtube & the TED website, the audio is terrible though. Anyway, a TEDx is great for branding and elevates your authority as a personal brand. Regardless of whether or not you make mistakes!

Then it was time for Rockstar Speaker Australia with my new close. Thankfully, this now worked! The marketing worked again, we had lines for Brisbane and Melbourne of people waiting to get in and we sold well too. We sold our retreat and we sold out quickly so we had to add more retreats. Finally both models were working and were now proven to work. We finished the year with two retreats, one in Sanctuary Cove and one in Bondi. These were 3 day events, luckily Les was responsible for most of the content as this was his jam. However in Sanctuary Cove I had to step up a bit and take on almost a whole day's worth of new content. This was important for me because I now proved to myself that I could do a premium event on my own, that perhaps I didn't need anyone else alongside me to make this work.

I ended 2019 with a holiday to Singapore and Japan and that wrapped up an incredible year.

What happens when an unstoppable train at full acceleration collides with a reinforced steel wall?

2020 comes along and at this stage my momentum is at an all time high, and my confidence is at an all time high. Like I always do, I take January off to work at the tennis in Brisbane and Melbourne and then I get back into it. With this new found confidence I thought, why don't I do an event on my own. I can do a half day event and then make the sale on the stage.

Up until this point I hadn't really been delivering the close. Reggie was driving the close when we did it together (I had some role but not much) and Les handled the close for Rockstar Speaker. I wanted to close now, let's see if I can do it on my own.

Where did I want to do the event? Let's go back to California. Los Angeles & Anaheim. I chose this because LA was great for me last time, probably the best financial result so far but also I wanted to see the Lakers play again, I hadn't been for 4 years and we just built a super team. That's the beauty about running your own events, you make your own rules. These events were scheduled in March, the ads were on and it was time to watch the numbers come through. They were branded differently, and thus Sold Out

Seminars was born.

Sign up was great, cost per lead was awesome. However the nature gods once again had other plans… Oh yeh, this thing called Covid. I narrowly avoided it, and I mean narrowly. About a week before the event the news started reporting that covid had hit Los Angeles. At this stage though the western world didn't really think too much of it and nothing was shut down, no one was losing their mind, yes there was serenity and calmness in 2020 if you can believe it. Do I cancel the event and not risk it or do I go? Ah you know me by now, nothing was going to stop me, all systems go let's do it. I get to LA and it's worse now, there was a case at the airport and the chatter is increasing. No restrictions yet. I go to the basketball to see the Lakers play in a packed out stadium on the second night that I get there and then it's time to prepare for the event.

First event was in LA. LA was starting to see an increase in the case numbers, the timing was really bad. We expected about 80-100 people. We had maybe 20 if we were lucky. Ouch, it was happening again. This time it was frustrating because it was me alone, I knew I could make it work, but the timing was just so unfortunate, it seems people in LA were starting to worry.

After this, my expectations were low for Anaheim. If LA had a low show up rate, 30 minutes down the freeway isn't going to change that. I thought this whole trip was going to be for nothing, which would be a major mental setback. However, Anaheim was packed. Absolutely packed, I couldn't believe it. I commanded the stage, the volume on the videos didn't work, and I couldn't care less, I was just happy to be doing it. No one else to rely on, no one to pick up slack if I messed up, it's all on me now. Time for the close - and yes that worked too. The Anaheim event more than made up for the failure in LA and boom I proved the model would work with me as the lone speaker.

I go back to LA, there's supposed to be another game on, I thought that maybe I would try to get tickets. Uh oh. Announcement: All NBA games have been suspended. This is serious now. I actually went to Universal Studios before I left, yes a theme park in the middle of a pandemic, maybe not the best idea, but I would do it again. The day after, a state of emergency was called in the US. I remember being at the hotel restaurant and Donald Trump was on TV announcing the state of emergency. Little did I know how much the world would change since then.

I got home just one day prior to the Australian government forcing mandatory quarantine on all international arrivals. Timing is everything, and perhaps this tour happened at just the right time.

The world stopped, but I couldn't stop. Not now. Not when I was so close to becoming a main fixture on the speaking circuit.

So what happens when an unstoppable train at full acceleration collides with a reinforced steel wall?

I was about to find out.

The train being me, the reinforced steel wall being covid and the lockdowns that ensued.

Here's the answer: the train always wins. Unstoppable forces always win. Full acceleration and momentum always wins. You need to be that unstoppable force, you need to find a way to win even if the path to winning seems unlikely or unclear. You make the path.

Covid changed my life, more for the better than the worse. It didn't mean I couldn't speak anymore, it just gave me new rules I had to abide by. Or new rules I could create into the model that was working.

I moved quickly. I got back in March when everything was going crazy, and then went live with my first online event in April. Everyone around me including my coaches were telling me how now was not the right time, you have to wait, nothing will work, everyone is freaking out, there's no point trying an online event. Reggie was more on the fence. He said you try it first, if it works I will jump in. But everyone else was still against the idea.

I've always trusted my gut instinct on timing. And this was no different. It wasn't just a good time to do this, it was the perfect time. 2020 was the perfect storm and you can bet I wasn't going to sit on my ass and wait for someone to do something for me. I'll make my own luck and I will make it work.

April comes around, it's time for the event. I only went for about 2 hours, and we had about 140 people in the audience. People said you can't sell at high ticket prices in 2 hours online with a cold audience. I said watch me. In 2 hours I made just over $40,000. No traveling, no expenses, just my computer and an internet connection. You bet I was over the moon. And it was easy. Now the model was proven online, on my own, with less expenses and no longer bound by geographical constraints. Higher profit margins, higher ROI, more time for me to do what I want and service the clients too. The unstoppable force always wins.

I planned two events per week ongoing for the next few months, and I hit some crazy goals. In May from memory the revenue was $160,000 in just a month. I mean this was insane to me. An online business based on me talking and being able to pull in that kind of money was unheard of. I was trained to believe that was a good annual salary, let alone a month's salary, and all whilst wearing a Nike hoodie. Yes, I literally wore a Nike hoodie for most of my online events, my slides had different fonts and colors, my hair hadn't been cut in months, I was walking proof that you don't need to be polished to be profitable

The Tour Of Childhood Heroes & Idols

After what was now 6 months of live events, twice per week. It was now time to go to the next level. I had perfected my presentation and I had achieved 6 months straight of incredible results. Really mind blowing results that I didn't think were possible, albeit during a global pandemic too. I simply didn't slow down, I never allowed myself to slow down, I knew the payoff at the end would be worth it.

Enter phase B.

What was phase B?

Well my dream was to host massive events with celebrity speakers, just like the events I attended where Eric Thomas and then Gary V were the main speakers. Now that time has arrived. Yes we still couldn't do in person events, but online events were all the rage. To make matters even better, celebrity fees were cheaper because it was online and there were also no travel costs. This was a perfect and less risky way for me to test my presentation out to a larger audience without having to front up $100k+ just to put the event on.

This was it, I decided that I was going to do it. Now it was time to choose the speaker.

I wanted these events to mean something. I had gone from this little shy kid to now potentially working alongside some of my idols and heroes. Naturally I decided that I should try my best to secure an event with some of these people that I looked up to from a young age.

My thought was to make the event for an Australian crowd. In online events you convert better when you speak to a local audience (which is the opposite for in person events funnily enough). When I think of business in Australia, I think of Mark Bouris.

Mark Bouris was the host of The Apprentice & The Celebrity Apprentice in Australia. He was the 'you're fired' guy over here. From a young age I remember always watching that show and admired his unwavering confidence, I always wanted to be like that. So I feverishly tried to find out how to book him to speak, what his fees were, how do I even get in contact with someone who can help me do this. I get to the person and we go back and forth for a while, and for whatever reason it falls through. Damn, I thought, clearly I'm too young, new or something just isn't right. I had spent a good 2 months trying to lock this in.

I can't lie I was feeling a bit down here because now I wasn't sure if anyone would want to do the event with me. On to my next target: Eric 'ET' Thomas.

The first event I ever went to see someone speak was ET. Actually I went twice, the first time I even got a photo with him. This was the guy that whenever he was in Australia I made sure to get tickets. I was only maybe 16 or 17 at the time I first saw him speak, it was early in his career when he launched his first book. ET had a massive impact on me, I remember watching his videos every Monday as I was vying to make it in tennis and he was an epic motivational speaker. He had worked with the best of the best in the NBA and a variety of companies.

Well to my surprise, ET said yes.

Of course I needed to pay him, well I would say I had the pleasure to pay him. Because this was someone who gave me so much, and all I had given him really was what, bought a couple of tickets to his events and bought his books which was maybe $200 in total. I was more than happy to pay him what he was worth, which most, if you knew the fee, would consider it a high price tag.

I honestly thought he would be harder to get than the Australian speakers. ET is an international speaker and has a massive profile. I started telling some of my high up colleagues and they were like what the heck, how did you get ET, is this serious or are you being scammed?

Well, it was very serious. And it was happening. October 2020 Ethan Donati & Eric Thomas, was this real life?

I remember being a nervous wreck for this event. ET signs into the zoom I see him on video and that's when I know, oh ok this is really happening. I even shared the story of how I came to know him, showed some photos of us back in the day and it was just a really awesome time. To this day I think ET is my favorite celebrity I have worked with because he was so generous and you could tell he really loved being with the audience, giving everything he had and the crowd loved it. I think we had maybe 600 people. Yes 600 people live, which was massive, we were used to 100 people if that.

All in all, the event financially wasn't the best result, in fact I may have even lost money overall, but that's besides the point, I had achieved part of my dream. I had worked so hard to the point where I was now speaking & producing an event alongside one of my heroes that I grew up admiring. I went from attending his events, to producing the events that invite him to speak. It was really happening, This was real.

Although I lost money, I am very resourceful, I used the event to attract other benefits that aren't only money related. Things like relationships and connections. In fact I used this event to invite another of my childhood role models to speak, Owen Cook. Owen was the main person that I was learning from about how to become better socially during high school when I was my most socially awkward. This is someone that had such a profound impact on my life, here was my way to give back. He is a very influential person too, we're talking millions of Youtube views. He accepted the invite and since that day we have still been friends. I also couldn't believe he was there and even talking to me on the phone the days leading up to it. I literally get nervous speaking to him, well not anymore, but I used to, he was literally one of my first ever role models. Now he is inviting me to hang out at his Hollywood mansion.

Who was next? Which big name speaker was I going to plan an event with next?

What do you mean who was next, didn't you say you lost money why would you do it again?

Because I'm crazy. Kidding, kinda, because instead of freaking out about losing money like 99% of people, I analyzed it, strategized why it went wrong and addressed it. Just like an engineer, find problem, fix problem, try the next iteration. Of course this is an expensive way to find problems, but the quicker you learn the quicker you get to your destination.

So naturally I reached out to Gary V. Of course that was the dream, but his price tag was out of my reach.

The speaker I did get for the next event was someone I thought I would never ever get the chance to speak to, let alone produce an event and speak alongside.

This was someone who was basically the pioneer of modern day marketing, he essentially created email marketing in the commercial sense and is one of the most known authors in the marketing space, if you know him, you know him, he needs no introduction:

Seth Godin.

Yes, Seth Godin.

If you don't know who he is, I recommend you do a Google search and get some of his books.

I never in 100 years would have imagined this would happen. But it was. it was expensive and it was risky, but it was also time. Say yes, figure out how later.

This event I planned completely differently, and I will talk about how to plan these events for the best result as a producer and as a speaker later on in the how to section. I used this event to create a relationship with another speaker, Aaron Sansoni. Aaron was actually the speaker at the first ET event I went to that was selling the program. I thought he would be good to get for the event from a promoter stand point. That also turned out to be a great long term relationship, he ended up being my client, still is to this day for what is now over a year. Aaron even allowed us to use his studio for the event which is a fantastic facility.

Before the event, I was given a 10 minute one on one conversation with Seth to plan for the event. I had to contain my excitement and try my best to remember to keep calm. But that was huge, I got to speak to Seth Godin one on one, incredible.

Well it was time. My biggest event ever. Not only as a speaker, but I advertised the event, I got the people to sign up and I produced the event. I don't know anyone else who is the producer, the marketer and the speaker of the event - this also gives me an uncanny advantage. We logged in and to my disbelief there were 3,000+ people there and yes it was live.

3,000 people!! From all over the world. It was game time!

And what an event it turned out to be. I did a Q&A with Seth Godin, I had 2 hours up there on my own too and it was just a tremendous event. This time despite it being more expensive, it turned out to be profitable.

What a rush. I had a new found sense of confidence, of possibility and of drive.

This event would also end up opening more doors for me that I imagined at the time too. More connections, more respect and the ability to charge more too. I ended up meeting Joel Bauer through this event and gaining some serious credibility in the speaker industry. A couple of days later I searched online and someone had written a whole blog post about the event, people were tweeting about things I said too, it was just like woah, where is this all coming from.

We had time in the year for one more celebrity event. This time we did get an Australian speaker - Naomi Simson.

Naomi is someone else I look up to. She is from the TV Show: Australian Shark Tank, the 'red shark'. She also gave the speech at my graduation ceremony from University. An inspiring woman and really knowledgeable too. We had a great conversation before the event on our one on one convo and a great Q&A during the event, all smiles and all love from the crowd.

Even though I had done two of these now, the novelty of being able to speak to these celebrities and work alongside them was not lost on me. It was really surreal still, and even people around me were just so surprised at how fast I was moving and excelling.

This time we focused on having less people at the event but making it only an Australian audience to see if the results would change at all. We had about 300 on live, and to prove my hypothesis of having higher conversion rates for a local audience online, the conversion rate went up. So I was making more sales with less people because they were more of the right audience for what I offer.

And that was the end of 2020. What a year business wise and personal wise I got to work alongside my heroes.

It wasn't all smooth sailing there were lots of tough events, some that didn't go to plan or that operated at a loss. Then there was the issue that my Facebook account got shut down and to this day I still haven't been able to get it back. Facebook asked me to verify my ID but they wouldn't even accept it. I'm not talking about having the Facebook ads banned, no, I couldn't login to my own personal account. All my data was lost overnight.

Now for most people this sounds trivial. But remember that my whole business is Facebook marketing, advertising for events, advertising for clients - all of this happens on Facebook. Losing it was potentially losing my whole business. Luckily backups were in place, contingencies were in plan and you never would have noticed that anything went down. If you can make even the mistakes look planned you're in good shape, same as when you are on stage speaking.

2020 was insane but there was still one thing missing though…

My dream of producing and speaking at my own in person celebrity event…

6

The Year of Dreams

"I ran out of tears when I was eighteen
So nobody made me but the main streets
'Cause too many people think they made me
Well if they really made me, then replace me"
- The Weeknd, Sidewalks

I start 2021 with being awarded a 2 Comma Club award. This was an award I have wanted for years, ever since I saw them being handed out in 2017. I remember when these awards first came out and how it seemed that whoever won one of them seemed like they must have their whole life figured out and that they really 'made it' in business.

The award is for earning one million dollars through one funnel using a software called Clickfunnels. It was basically the award every personal brand and online entrepreneur wants to earn. I had finally done it after years of aiming for it. I remember the day it arrived at my house, unpacking it and having it up right next to my bedroom door so every single day I would walk past it and it would fill me with a sense of pride. Something I had never really felt about business before this. It was a constant reminder I was on the right path and I was realizing my dreams, however unrealistic they once were.

The funny thing is though, once I had that award, I felt like I could do more, I could do even better. Once I got it I realized well actually that wasn't THAT hard. It's doable. This is another huge lesson that is hard to put into words. Your expectations set your results. I always thought earning one million was something excruciating and hard to do, I never even considered I could do more than one million. Once I earned it though, my expectations changed. They went higher. And so what took me years to win my first million dollar award and a year to make that revenue, the next time only took me a week.

Yes, one week.

Some of my clients have done it in a day so this is what I mean by expectations and relative goals, for me one week was very achievable because I had seen so many people I work with do it in a single day (2 hours even).

Set your goals and expectations higher. Watch what happens. Whatever you think is possible or just past possible, raise the bar a little bit higher, force yourself to get better. Even be around and actively search for people doing more than you so you know there is another level and that is right in your face.

So how did I do it in a week? Let me tell you the story...

The Seven Figure Week

> *"If you're going to be a fucking rock star, go be one. People don't want to see the guy next door on stage; they want to see a being from another planet."*
>
> *- Lemmy Kilmister*

There were so many variables that contributed to this epic week. I'll do my best to include all of them.

Essentially it was time to live my dream. My dream of putting on an in person tour with a headline celebrity speaker. Keep in mind this is still early 2021, with the pandemic still very much causing havoc.

When I decided to launch a tour in April 2021 I heard all of the same doubts from other people just like I had heard in April 2020 when launching the online events. It was bad timing, they told me, don't do an in person event, especially across states it's too risky they said, borders could close, outbreaks could occur, venues could get shut down, planes could get canceled, you could even catch covid. Like I said, I've always trusted myself when it comes to timing. In fact I was advised to do another tour in November 2021 and I said no because the timing was not right, and I was correct, everyone else's tours got pushed back because of lockdowns.

Well for this one I was pretty confident. It was maybe late January when I started planning, and here in Australia there really weren't many cases at all and there were no mandates. All the states were open to each other and I was confident it would stay like that. I was also confident that people wanted to go to events, there had been no business events of this size in over a year and there was no one putting on public events like this.

You know me, I always have to be different.

And so I was crazy enough to do it. Not only to do it but to pull it off.

In person events are much more complex than online and much more expensive. Let's go through the process of what had to be done.

First things first, we needed to secure a guest speaker. I still wanted to work with Mark Bouris. So that's who I went for. He already rejected me once before, but now I had the proof and I had other celebrities that had worked with me. After some back and forth over a month or two, we had an agreement. Looking back through my emails, I started this process in November 2020 and we got it over the line in February 2021, three months to secure him as a speaker.

Then they sent me the speaker fee and all the costs involved and that's when I knew, ok we aren't in Kansas anymore, this is the big leagues now. This was a big gamble, but one I was willing to take.

I knew we had to produce a show, this couldn't just be a little local event like we were used to doing. We needed to make people feel like this was a proper event. At the same time though I wasn't worried or pressured to add the bells and whistles. All I needed was an audience, a venue and an offer and I knew it would be fine.

7

The Play by Play

The Concept

I am a straight shooter, Mark is a straight shooter, the world we were in had created tough times for a lot of business owners, but at the same I didn't want them feeling sorry for themselves. This was supposed to be a driving force to help them get back on their feet, not a pity party. So I decided on the name of the event to be: Adapt Or Die.

Controversial, divisive and polarizing, just the style I was going for. Here is a great tip, the more polarizing you can be the more you will attract your ideal audience. I didn't want people who were offended by the name to be at my event, they weren't the right fit for me. I wanted people who had ambition and were prepared for some honest truth. Have some showmanship about your events, make every thing you do create some sort of feeling in the audience. Alienate those that are not right for you so that you will be loved by the ones who are.

We even had a few people get angry at us for the name. People we didn't even know on social media either message the page or comment on the ads that the name was too full on. For them I'm sure it was. Like I said though, they aren't for me. Be you and attract your ideal client, don't go begging to anyone who will like you and in the process you lose all sense of your real identity just to please others.

The Strategy

My plan sounded simple: have 300 people per city attend. We would go to Brisbane, Melbourne & Sydney so 3 cities, 900 people. Initially I expected to be at a massive loss after advertising. Usually with events you spend more money to get someone to buy the ticket for the event than you make per ticket sale. It makes me laugh when people think event organizers get rich selling tickets for $97 or $297. No, events usually operate at a loss. This made it hard to plan for exact numbers in terms of costs involved as we wouldn't really find out how much it cost per ticket sale until we started running some of the ads.

I had the plan, now I needed the venues. In any other circumstance the event venues would have been extremely hard to acquire, but because we were in a pandemic with literally no events for a year the venues were basically available whenever we wanted. I always recommend going for the best venues. It adds more legitimacy, which helps with show up rate and sales rate. The other good news was that because of the pandemic the venues were actually at a discounted rate too. We went to the convention centers in Melbourne & Brisbane and The Star in Sydney. If you can ever do an event at The Star I would really recommend it. Do not go for cheaper venues to save a few dollars, it will cost you more in the end.

We had the celebrity, the venues and the plan of what we wanted to achieve. However there was another issue: my presentation and offer. Arguably the most important part, without this, there is no return on investment and I would end the tour with a massive loss. Now you might be thinking, what do you mean, you have done presentations for ages why would this be different? Well my presentation I had been doing prior to this event was only aimed at speakers and coaches.

This event was not for speakers and coaches, it was for business owners. Mark Bouris is one of the biggest business authorities in the country, he is going to be attracting the heavy hitting business owners. For the most part these business owners also had much more experience than me, and in fact I was still one of the youngest business owners in the room. I had to overcome that limiting belief in the audience but also I had to revamp my presentation. I couldn't exactly tell a fencing business owner that he should go and become a speaker and coach now could I?

I turned to Cherie. She sat down with me, gave me some great advice and over about a week I dramatically changed my presentation. Which brings me to the next point, and I do not recommend this, but I didn't actually practice the presentation before the tour. What's more is I hadn't presented a sales presentation at an in person event for over a year so I wasn't well versed heading into this tour. There is a huge difference between speaking on your laptop with your slides right there to look at the whole time versus on a stage where you are facing the audience and can't see the slides for the most part.

Keep in mind after speaker costs and venue costs the bill was already over $120,000. This wasn't exactly a small amount of money to test out a whole new presentation to an audience that I was not used to selling to.

To mitigate that risk I had to think like a promoter not only as a speaker. Like I said earlier, it's uncommon that one person is the promoter, speaker and marketer for the event. These are usually all different people. I put my promoter hat on and said who could I get to speak as well as me so that when they sell I get a portion of their sales and therefore even if I do terribly, their sales will cover the costs of the event? That's when I brought Aaron back, he speaks to business owners all the time, he knows what he is doing, I brought him in to mitigate my risk and cover the costs of the event.

At this point though we hadn't sold any tickets yet so I needed to get on to that, it could have been awkward otherwise. This is my thing, it's what I do, I fill up events. Pass me the ball and I will handle the rest.

Do you know when I know how a campaign is going to be successful? When the ads get hate. Some of these ads got hate because of the name, we even had one person say 'why don't you just call it "adapt"?' When I started seeing these ridiculous comments, I knew it was going to go well.

I aimed for 300 tickets per city so 900 total and out of 900 I anticipated 100 VIP tickets. Prices were $47-97 for general and $197-297 for VIP. We ended up selling 1,572 tickets and 435 of them were VIP. We far exceeded what I was aiming for, a huge win. This is always the biggest variable to me - will people actually sign up and show up? I know that if I have an audience I will do well. I don't get nervous about speaking or what am I going to say on stage, I get nervous about whether people will actually show up. I know that once they are there I will blow them away.

I was expecting us to lose money on the ads to sell tickets, however we ended up spending $106,000 on advertising and making $192,000 in ticket sales. This meant we now had a budget to use for the bells and whistles and the pressure was reduced a little bit. We could have gone into the event down $250,000 instead we were only down maybe $90,000.

The majority of the tickets were sold from Facebook & Instagram ads, I also ran some Google & Youtube ads along with having an Eventbrite set up for the event too. Overall we had roughly 30 unique ads that we rotated throughout two months of advertising, depending on which were working better at different times.

At the completion of someone buying a ticket, I set up a survey of specific questions for them to answer. This serves multiple purposes. Firstly it gives us more information so we can tailor the event to the people there, it also tells us if we are attracting the right audience, it gives us the ability to follow up people who may want marketing help and it also gives the audience a bigger sense of buy-in. It's a more emotional and mental investment which means they are more likely to attend and take it seriously.

I had set up a daily tracking system so I could see every single day how many tickets were sold, how much we spent on ads and all of the main metrics that I need to look at to know when to change things up. These daily metrics included cost per ticket sale, total revenue from ticket sales, profit loss per day, breakdown of VIP vs General Admission tickets sold per day and click through rate for the ads. By updating these daily I was able to track any trends, which would let me know if the ads needed to be changed.

This whole event relied on the advertising, I think people forget that. Without the ads there is no audience, I couldn't care who is speaking or where the event is, if there is no audience there is nothing. Everything rides on marketing and advertising. Some of the days we operated at a loss, especially at the start, instead of freaking out, we understood that sometimes marketing needs time to start operating at its best. You have to be able to see things in terms of trends and longer term data, not just one day here or there.

Apart from the ads we also had to make the event into a show. We needed some merchandise to brand our event and give it that extra sense of legitimacy. We bought a huge banner for the stage, if you look at my site or any of the videos about the event you will see the banner, branded booklets, branded pens, T-shirts, lanyards and we had hired 20 staff over the three events to come in and help out. It was a lot of effort to get these done and organize the logistics of it all. Our team was small too. Essentially it was just me and Taryn. Behind the scenes my parents also helped out with organizing some of the lanyards and packing the books. Small teams can sometimes be the best.

Taryn has worked for me since the beginning of the Sold Out Seminars events and she has a lot of contact with the clients as well as organizing logistics. She is an essential part to the business for the client facing side of things as well as in the backend creating funnels and ads. She was in charge of organizing all of these branded items and she did a flawless job. Everything looked extremely professional, was produced perfectly and arrived at all the venues on time.

We did have issues with our lanyard provider who twice mistakenly sent us incorrect versions of our lanyards. Instead of having a blank space for someone to write their own name, the lanyard came back with "name goes here" printed where the blank space was supposed to be. Thankfully they managed to get us the correct version about two days before the event.

To be clear for a free event or a smaller event you don't need any of this at all. At my free events I would just have myself, one other person helping out and none of the branded stuff at all. Literally anyone can do a small free event on their own whereas for larger scale events you need a team to help out.

This event we also had an MC, usually you wouldn't need one but because we had multiple speakers and a whole day full of content, I wanted someone to be able to tie together the whole event. The best person to use for an MC is actually someone that has worked with you and gone through your process. I fortunately had a client, Leanne, who is a professional speaker and teaches other speakers how to be better speakers too. She also has a speakers bureau and she had great results from working with us. So it was a no brainer to have Leanne be the MC, and she graciously accepted. She was fantastic during the event, she had the crowd on their feet, engaged and ready to learn.

I also like to choose MC's and speakers based on fit. For example I am a very dense speaker, I go fast and there is a lot of information. I am more of a 'transactional' speaker. You'll leave my presentation with a sore hand from writing too many notes, you will leave overwhelmed and possibly confused too. When I choose speakers for my events to complement my style they need to be more 'transformational' speakers so that the crowd can have a bit of a rest and some feel good humor or emotions. Aaron as the other speaker is more transformational so that is a good fit, Mark is similar to me, a very dense information rich speaker. So we already had three males, two very dense and one transformational, I needed more balance. Leanne is also a transformational speaker and female so that balances the day more. I also added one more portion, that is the 'repitch'.

The repitch was another backup plan of mine. The repitch is something made popular by Myron Golden, a fantastic speaker who I recently had as a guest to my premium three day event. Essentially it is when someone makes a repitch of your offer after you make it. For example if I make an offer in the morning, someone else with a different voice and different perspective to me comes on and repitches my offer. For this I had Taryn. She had always wanted to be a speaker and she knows my process inside and out so I wanted to give her the chance to go on stage. She was understandably nervous as it was really her first time on stage apart from her TEDx talk, but on a stage like this it was her first time. She did great and in fact didn't even need to repitch at all. Taryn also had the role of being operations manager for the event, keeping all the staff on task and managing the AV and venue staff to ensure all the bells and whistles went off without a hitch. She was the person I could rely on to do all of that whilst I focused on doing what I do.

The final considerations for the event was to now focus on getting people to show up. We did this with email marketing: sending out personalized tickets, instant confirmation emails and lead up emails with location information and maps. We also hired assistants to call every single person who bought a ticket. The additional hiring of staff and the merchandise elements really added unexpected costs to the event as well. I am someone who is very transparent, unlike most speakers and personal brands I have no problem sharing numbers.

Going into the event we had spent roughly $270,000 and made $196,000. So I was down $74,000 before stepping foot into the venue. It can sound intimidating but at this stage I knew I had the audience, my most important element. Calculating the numbers in my head I concluded that even if only 1,200 of the 1,456 show up and Aaron closes 10% of the audience, I get a portion of that, which will already more than cover my costs. Even if I absolutely bombed out and no one bought I would still be breakeven, and that gave me peace of mind.

The final element before the event was making sure the room dynamics were correct. I learned room dynamics from Les, he was adamant that this was perhaps the most important part of an event, he came from a rockstar background so he was all about the performance. He always said you need to make the room feel full, it needs to feel packed, like an arena, atmosphere is everything.

So we planned for 70% attendance and only put out 70% of the chairs, with the rest on standby. That way if more turned up, we would add more chairs which would look very good optically, and if less attended well it still wouldn't look as empty. Better to have to add chairs than have to remove them. VIP's had their own area at the front and it was clearly separated from the general admission area.

The next part with room dynamics is having the area for sales tables. They should be inside the room, never have them outside. This is because as the speaker you can gauge how you are performing by the amount of people running to the back but more importantly it acts as social proof as other attendees are seeing other people buy which reinforce their decision to also buy. We had our sales area in a horseshoe shape so the staff could stand behind the desks and have everything they needed. Again if you are doing a smaller event you can just have a couple of tables at the back instead of a larger area. There also need to be walkways between the seats so people can easily get up and walk to the back.

The structure of the day was also planned strategically. The MC would go up first, get the crowd excited and ready to go. I then went on for about 2-2.5 hours. The first half an hour was content only, and then I transitioned into my sales presentation. I made the first offer, which can be a good or bad thing. It can be good because you are the first offer they see for the day which means they haven't spent their money on anything else. The risk though is, they may get offended if they didn't expect a sale or a sale so soon, or they may wait to see who else makes an offer to them that day. The other consideration is the framing. Once they are primed to buy they are actually more likely to buy later on. So the fact I have got the audience ready to buy, means the other speakers after me may also benefit.

Then we went on a short break, and I came back on stage after the break. Why? Firstly, it confirms that they made the right decision. When people make a purchase sometimes they go through what's called cognitive dissonance. Which essentially means they are unsure if they made the right decision. Most speakers just sell and then run away. Which only makes this worse. Instead I went on for another 90 minutes with more content, actually more advanced content to show them that yes you made the right choice, and all of this is included in what you already bought anyway. I did make a soft close for a marketing event, but this was like a five minute offer and it was more to bundle it with Aaron's coming up next.

Then we would go to the main lunch break. When we got back, I planned that it would take some time for people to get back in the room. Taryn then spoke for about 20 minutes after the lunch break. She was also doing a repitch for my sale, reaffirming those that already bought and holding the room until most had returned from lunch. Then I introduced Aaron to come on stage, he would go for about two hours and would make his offer. Me introducing him allowed me to transfer the relationship I had already built with the audience onto him. Finally it would be Mark Bouris on for 45 minutes and I would join him on stage to moderate a 15 minute Q&A. At the end of this the MC would wrap it up, and the VIPs plus those that bought my offer were invited to the VIP one hour session with me where I then went into the most advanced content plus did a Q&A. The VIP session was great to once again reaffirm those that bought but also the Q&A showed a different side of me which results in more people buying after that session too, although I did not make an offer.

You always want to have the drawcard celebrity last, otherwise you will lose large portions of the crowd before you even make an offer. If you are having a VIP session make sure it is after the entire event and that anyone that bought from you also gets to attend.

With everything set in motion, there was only one thing that could derail me now, covid. About 3 or 4 weeks prior to the tour, Brisbane had a small outbreak of cases. They actually went into lockdown. Luckily it ended up being only a 3 or 5 day lockdown and then they got a handle on the cases and everything was fine again. We were actually extremely lucky timing wise. Just before the tour there were small outbreaks but just after in May there were lockdowns and more outbreaks again. We pulled off a needle in a haystack.

The Tour

Leading up to the tour it was getting exciting as all of the material we ordered was arriving at the house and it was all becoming very real. Over four months of planning were about to culminate in three events over 7 days and then it would all be over just like that. My mind was racing with things that may go wrong - what if there is an outbreak, what if Mark or I get sick, what if someone pulls out at the last minute. All of these negative thoughts did enter my mind, I just wanted to get to April 19th as quickly as possible.

NO ONE'S COMING

Before the event we went to visit the Melbourne venue. I recommend this because you want to know exactly what you are walking into. How does the room look, what is the setup like, can you see everything etc. We also did the same once we arrived in Brisbane & in Sydney.

But the week before the tour I was invited to speak at Aaron's premium event which was in Perth. This was supposed to be on April 16 and Adapt or Die was April 19. Most people may not have done it, especially with the added risk. What if there was an outbreak in Perth and I had to be isolated? I think looking back it was a bigger risk than necessary but I did end up going. The reasons being I had never been to Perth before, I also hadn't spoken in person to an audience for ages and I needed all the practice I could get, so for me it was a mini warm up. I wasn't selling at the Perth event, I was just presenting, so there was no pressure, a good practice run and it was the same kind of audience I would be speaking to at Adapt Or Die, seasoned business owners. It was also a good distraction to take my mind off the tour, so I went and did it and it was all smooth.

I get back to Melbourne, raring to go, but clearly the stress has gotten to me. I break out in hives all over my body. I had never experienced anything like it, itchy all over, overheating, it was all happening. I had to get plenty of cream and supplements to try to calm this thing down. This was my body giving into the stress and anxiety of what I was about to do. It was my name on the event, on the ads, on the day, if something wasn't good it would come back to me. I was worried that I would freeze up there or that I would look stupid or that the business owners wouldn't take me seriously because I was much younger than the average. Essentially all my old limiting beliefs came back to the surface, which meant this was another success ceiling.

Unlike the last success ceiling I had which showed up by me breaking down in the airport on the way to Colorado, this success ceiling showed by my body breaking out in hives. It was never going to stop me, yes it was extremely uncomfortable, but this was the big game. I had Jos, my videographer come down to Melbourne (and also Sydney) and I had 400+ people that were about to attend this event. All I needed was an audience, someone at the back to take sales and I was fine. Everything else around me was stressing me out. Usually I keep very calm and to myself during events. This time was harder, people needed things from me, they needed to clarify things with me and the energy of that combined with the uncertainty of what was to come absolutely stressed me out and changed my usual state of calm and relaxed.

Event #1: Melbourne

We go to the event venue the day before, get all of the VIP books together and have everything ready for the day tomorrow, yes I get my hands dirty too. It takes about two hours to do all of this and we realize how much there is here. We plan for tomorrow and fingers crossed people show up.

It's the event day and people were definitely showing up. We had to add more staff in the reception area and tell them to move quicker because there was a massive line building of attendees waiting. We didn't want to keep them waiting and we had to start on time. After the reception team got into a groove I went up to the green room on my own and just tried to get out of my head and relax. I was first on after the MC introduction and I was feeling the anxiety. It got to a point where I was like maybe I just don't even make an offer, no need to embarrass yourself, no one is going to buy, it's all good, Aaron will sell and you won't lose $80k. My brain was racing at 1000 miles per hour. However, I was about to overcome the success ceiling.

I needed a calming influence to talk to so I sent a quick message to Joel Bauer about 10 minutes before I'm due on stage. I didn't know if he would see it, but he did. Joel and I have a special relationship, we started out as him being a guest speaker to my audience and then he became a client of mine and I still run his online marketing campaigns. Joel is the top trainer of online income earners. He has trained the best of the best: Dan Lok, Peng Joon, Russell Brunson, he basically has trained the who's who of online marketers.

He is the original expert of this. He is there for me as a mentor which I am very grateful for.

He has such a unique way of speaking and I have never met anyone with such genuine desire to be there for people. In true Joel fashion, he doesn't only reply to my text he video calls me and I immediately smile, there was the stress relief just when I needed it. I went from thinking 'do I really need to be the one on the stage, can't I just stay behind the scenes' to 'ok here is what I was made to do, let's not lose sight of that.'

He doesn't give me a motivational pep talk, he gives me a calm reassuring voice and basically tells me to stop being selfish, it's nothing to do with me, I have done the work now it's time to help those that have attended. Immediately my stress washes away, I feel my shoulders get lighter and I feel more excitement than nervousness for the first time. There are two minutes to show time, so I quickly make my way down to the backstage area.

I peek out of the door and see a packed room, and then my name is called, it's time to go on stage. I remember taking a second to take it all in and get my bearings. It was a big stage. This was it, I had produced an event that felt just the same as the event I went to as an attendee that inspired all of this in the first place, I was actually doing it.

My thinking brain gets turned off and I go into speaker mode, blasting the crowd with this fired up energy, everyone is glued to their seat. The audience is feverishly taking down notes, everyone is focused and that is the sign of a great performance. I jump off the stage, interact with the audience and spend most of the time off stage walking around in the crowd.

Melbourne was the worst in terms of room dynamics. We had social distancing still so the chairs were spaced out which made it look a bit weird and gave the empty feel that Les always warned against. Plus the projector was too big and covered by parts of the banner at the back. What's worse is the AV team put the music on way too low of a volume so there were awkward moments to start the event. Overall I do believe the room dynamics cost sales. At least we knew what to fix for the next events.

It is time now for me to make the offer. Yes I do feel somewhat nervous here. It is the first time using this close. Literally it is a new structure for me and one I have not yet practiced. Nothing like the real thing to use as practice hey?

So I ask the audience who would be interested to work with me and about half put their hands up, ok not bad. I go to start my close, and my close always starts with a video testimonial from Joel Bauer. It is an incredible testimonial where he says that if I were a woman he would marry me and propose. It usually has the crowd laughing and also seeing the power of what I do plus the care and relationship I have with clients.

I get to the slide with the video… I press 'Play'

White screen.. Hmm that's odd

I press back, I press play again. White screen again. Shit. I had removed the video from the slides and not changed over the slide deck. What a day for this to happen I thought, up there feeling nervous and strange as it is and then the one thing I can rely on to do its job isn't there.

One of Joel's principles is whatever goes wrong, make it seem normal. One time his whole computer shut down during his close and he just had a blue screen. So I took this as a test, a challenge if you will. An expensive lesson if it failed.

I kept going, made it seem normal and natural, explained the offer then I said the price. $4,995.

"To get it, go to the back of the room and sign up"

No one moves.

Ahh well, I guess at least I tried right. At that moment it was almost a feeling of relief more than anything, I thought ok at least I made an offer, if no one wants it that's fine I will improve for the next one.

I keep going though as I will train you to do, you never stop after the first price reveal. I keep talking and still no one is moving. I still have the feeling of being nervous, and when I am nervous on stage I am more passive. I don't go for it as much, I kind of sit back and hope.

But then, I see one guy get up. I was like oh hell yes. Even though it was one person, to me this was a moment I wanted for years, just to see one person get up to go to the back was huge for me. One person wanted to buy.

Oh actually no he didn't, he just went to the door, he is leaving for the break. But just as he left, another person stood up and he went to the tables. He was signing!! He was buying!!!

That gave me the confidence and boom I turned into my normal self. I went harder, had confidence in my voice and had conviction in my offer just like I was used to doing. I needed to go through this to find my way again.

Person after person stood up and went to the back. I kept going and going, until all of a sudden there was a huge amount of people, the tables were flooded at the back. It was unlike anything I had experienced before. I was doing what I once admired others for doing. Instead of being the attendee buying the program, I was the speaker selling the program. And the audience loved it.

I walk off the stage, Leanne follows me out, and I can't even describe the feeling. We were both like oh my god. It felt like 5 minutes of no one going to buy and then they all just went. It was relief, ecstasy, disbelief and exhilaration all rolled into one. Over 40 people bought. Forty six in the end!! That's over a ten percent close rate to a completely cold audience which is extremely difficult to do. The whole tour was now paid for, all my stress, all my worries were gone no matter what I did from here on in I couldn't lose. I had broken through my biggest success ceiling to date and had achieved my biggest accomplishment to date.

I cannot explain the jubilation and emotion that followed. I immediately went to the green room and I just remember having this feeling of disbelief. I was over the moon, full of energy, bouncing off the walls. Imagine having one of your biggest dreams come true after pushing through so much effort and sacrifice to get there. It really was like winning a championship in sports.

During the break I walked out to the main room and some of the audience were still there. I am not one of those speakers that avoids the audience, even though I feel uncomfortable around people still I am probably one of the only speakers that doesn't just avoid and stay away after they speak. I still feel like I am one of the audience members myself sometimes! The amount of people that came up to me and shared such nice words during the lunch break was so touching. I remember all of the interactions, that's also how my brain works, I do remember everyone's face I spoke to and roughly what was said. Social interactions in small settings do heighten my emotions because of the stress I encounter during them so I do have a stronger memory of everyone I speak to. A lot were Greek and my mum is Greek so we had a lot of connections and just a great time with those that were there.

I then spend the rest of the event mostly in the green room, coming in and out sometimes here and there. I was still nervous though. Although I had done great and everything was incredible, the result was much better than expected, I was nervous for one more thing. Meeting Mark Bouris.

I hadn't met him before, we hadn't spoken and some people had told me he wasn't the most social celebrity that they had worked with. For me that was understandable and also relatable because I am not the most social person either. But this was someone who I looked up to, my concern was what if he didn't like me or found something I say or do offensive. See I have all these limiting beliefs too, success doesn't mean you need to be perfect.

Anyway he gets there and I can hear my heart beating out of my chest. He walks in and it does feel a little odd, not much eye contact, no hand shake (I guess it is covid), he walks to the couch and sits and does his thing. Yes I am thinking that he must hate me. At the same time though I know that I am probably the exact same way, so it's actually comforting that neither of us feels the pressure nor need to try to be overly social or put on a front. I felt like we have a similar temperament.

Anyway it was time for him to get up there on stage. I jump on to do a Q&A with him at the end. Massive moment for me, standing on stage with Mark Bouris. We finish it up, he heads back to the airport and Melbourne is done. We pack it up and head over to Brisbane.

Event #2: Brisbane

Melbourne was great, however there were lots of issues with tech, with room set up and with staffing that needed to be addressed for the next two events. With those things fixed, who knew what result we might achieve for the next two events.

We arrived at the venue the day before, sorted all of the AV issues and room dynamics issues as best we could and I made sure to fix my presentation to include the video I needed. Same prep as in Melbourne, we're used to this now. Thankfully my hives had pretty much gone down as the stress had been relieved.

THE PLAY BY PLAY

Time for the event.

Brisbane had a much better event room than Melbourne. The chairs didn't need to be socially distanced so it was packed, and if you see the photos it looks packed too. We had to add a lot of chairs and had a bit over 400 attendees from memory. This time our staff were much quicker on the registration which meant no one was waiting too long. The only thing I didn't like was that the stage was quite small compared to Melbourne's. Nevertheless the room dynamic was a million times better and you could feel the buzz. This was a completely new atmosphere. I also had a few business friends who attended, including Marcus, that knew me around 2018/2019 when I wouldn't talk to anyone, in fact they were also at the first Dream Team event so they knew where I had come from. It was good to have some familiar faces to hang out with as well afterward.

Brisbane is also a less skeptical crowd than Melbourne. They are more enthusiastic generally and that's why we usually see a higher show up rate and an engaged atmosphere whereas Melbourne can be a bit quieter. I felt much more comfortable on stage now and gave one of my best performances. When it came to do the close, I didn't panic, I knew what to expect, no one would move for a bit and then there would be a couple going to the back and then there would be a stampede.

And that's exactly what happened.

I made the offer, no one got up. I was confident and calm. One person at the front gets up and walks to the tables, another one and another one, and then all of a sudden it seems that the whole room is up.

55 people ended up buying. Wow! Now I was getting close to a 15% close rate which is unheard of at these price points to a completely cold audience. Another incredible audience, a fantastic event and unbelievable result. I tell Taryn that there is no need to repitch, as our sales were way stronger than

expected, she could just speak without selling and then I get into the green room and chill out until Mark is set to arrive.

Now at this event we were a bit behind. For whatever reason over the course of the day we had gone over by a little bit we were maybe 20 minutes behind for Mark and he had a plane to catch. That was my only regret for this tour - that we were late, which meant Mark had to cut his time short a bit to make his plane in time and this made some of the audience unhappy. It also had Mark a bit frustrated understandably. This was probably the only rocky moment of the tour.

What contributed to the frustration of the audience before Mark, was that some of the audience told us they didn't really appreciate some of the sales techniques, it rubbed them the wrong way. There is a fine balance between result and crowd satisfaction as a promoter. For the speaker it doesn't really matter too much as they are more concerned with the result. But as the promoter you wear that blowback. Regardless of who was right or wrong, this was the first time I had ever had a complaint like that at an event.

Compared to Melbourne though, this was substantially better. All we could do now was fix the issue of being on time for Sydney's event and we may just have a perfect event.

Event #3: Sydney

It was fitting that Sydney was at the end. I initially thought Sydney would be the smallest event because it was lagging behind the other cities in terms of ticket sales. But in the last 2 weeks it really picked up and it was now the most sold event. We also had the best venue - The Star. This venue was incredible, hence why I wanted Jos to come up from Melbourne to get some footage.

This was what I imagined the dream event to look like. This wasn't just an event room, this was a theater. Proper chairs, a proper elevated stage, world class lighting and decorations. Then in the green room you had all the photos of famous people who had performed here. It was like a who's who of rock stars from all over the world. I think if this were the first event of the tour I would have been even more overwhelmed, now I embraced it.

I can't explain how incredible Sydney was. This was the perfect event. The professionalism, the venue, everything was just perfect. The AV team was a professional team and you could tell! They were used to producing theatrical events, this was a cakewalk for them.

I was warned that Sydney is a harder city to sell in. Well for me Sydney is the perfect audience. Usually it is the transformational speakers that find it more difficult because the Sydney audience is a no bullshit, straight shooter audience that are more 'left brain' inclined, like myself. They want the dense information, the how to, the step by step, that's my style of speaking. So when I am on they are taking all the notes in the world, because that's what they love. I had by far my best performance in Sydney of the whole tour. Sixty sales and the audience was only 400 people. A 15% close rate. Unbelievable.

The close was exactly the same, no one moved, then it just took one or two people to start the flow. Everything went off without a hitch. Well there was one massive hitch but it was completely out of our control.

It was Commbank. The bank we use to take payments. All of their merchant terminals went down which meant the sales team couldn't take a lot of the payments. It was all ok though in the end, I don't believe we lost sales from it, but that is probably the biggest thing that could go wrong is payment systems not working. Taryn was working feverishly to process the remainder of the payments manually after I was done. It was a mess, but handled.

Mark then arrives at the venue a bit before he is due to go on, and now that maybe we are a bit more comfortable with each other we have a conversation and we actually get on fine, our temperaments are quite similar and I think that is probably why he gets misunderstood by others as I have been too misunderstood for similar things. We are both much more relaxed at this event and we have a great time. He even extended his time on stage for this event, and everyone absolutely loved it.

By far we saved the best for last.

Overall I had a bit over 150 sales for the tour plus as the promoter I took a portion of Aaron's, so I collected well over one million dollars in just one week. I had lived out my dream for the first time. It's like winning a championship. You celebrate it, bask in it for a little bit but afterwards you know you still need to win more.

That's the beauty of platform speaking. I was making much more than the celebrity keynotes were and no one knew who I was. The celebrity would walk down the street and get stopped for photos and autographs, I can just walk, mind my own business, no one stops me or has a clue who I am. It's not only possible, it's the most lucrative and successful model for entrepreneurs that has stood the test of time. Can you start to see why and how this is so powerful for the everyday person who doesn't even have a public brand?

All of us in the industry probably owe a big thank you to Tony Robbins for normalizing the seminar industry business model. Even he started off by doing free events in LA when he was an unknown speaker. But make no mistake the event industry existed well before him too. It has stood the test of time and I believe it will continue to do so.

Unfortunately since this tour, covid took over and lockdowns ensued, borders were closed and mandates were imposed. So for now I don't know when the next time will be. Luckily I didn't listen to the advice to do it in November of 2021, what a nightmare that would have been. I had pulled off the perfect timing for the perfect concept of an event, I still don't think any other promoter put on a public event like that in Australia for all of 2021. It was funny how they were all telling me after the fact how obvious it was because everyone would have been dying to go out to an event. Hindsight is 20/20 I guess, but at the end of the day there was only one person crazy enough to try to pull it off and take the calculated risk.

The Final In Person Event & Hurdle of 2021

In May 2021 Aaron had a three day marketing event he wanted me to speak at. Not only speak at, but take on the majority of the event, roughly 7-8 hours of content per day. Now this was one of my oldest limiting beliefs I had to overcome. I was used to only doing events that were either free or very low cost for at most 4 or 5 hours at a time. Even at Rockstar Speaker retreat I didn't do most of the speaking, Les did. Yes I had one day where I took over and stepped up for a few hours that gave me the confidence to be the main speaker at a paid event but never on my own did I think I could hold a multi day premium event.

The three day event comes around, again I feverishly make enough content for the whole three day period. I still really am not sure as to how it will go or if I will even have enough for the three days. Turns out I can do a three day event without a problem. The audience was there from 8am to 8pm every day on average. Aaron spoke 2-3 hours per day and they had some breaks but the rest was me.

This gave me the final piece of confidence I needed to know for certain that I could facilitate a premium 3 day event and create all of the content for it. The feedback was phenomenal and again this was an event that gave me a rush just like Adapt Or Die did.

I decided to test my theory, and produce my own 3 day event, this time online, with people from all over the world. Now it was only me, my rules and created exactly how I wanted. From 9am to 6pm each day, the audience were there, engaged and learning. Not only that, over 20 of the attendees even gave me a video testimonial just about how good the event was.

Another skill was added to my arsenal as a speaker and this event was something I was so proud of because of how good and how much information it actually was. Most 3 or 4 day events just fill you with good emotions so you buy the next product and only teach you the 'what' and the 'why'. I'm a straight shooter, I don't pump your state with emotions, I tell you 'HOW' to do something, show you and then let you go and implement so you can come back and test how you went.

I now run these every quarter which you can find at www.milliondollarfunnelslive.com

This is the story, you have now experienced it, read it and hopefully picked up some nuggets of gold that you can apply to anything you do in business. You'll see I had the right support, I had a relentless will to win and I had used my pain to push me where most will never have the desire or discipline to go. You'll see I have the exact same, even more, limiting beliefs, negative thoughts and self doubts as most people do, and have had so through all stages of my career thus far and you'll see that if I can do this, literally anyone else can too.

II

The Stage is Yours

8

Your Stage Is Set

Well now let's transition.

Let's go from the story behind it, to the skills to do it. The 'how to' for you to be able to take the same or similar actions and try your hand at becoming a platform speaker. If you're genuine about wanting to have a business that works for you, platform speaking is the best way to do it. You spend less time selling and prospecting, which means you have more time to service your clients, more time to spend however you want in your daily life and more time to innovate.

Plus you get to visit the emotional heights that very few ever have the pleasure of hitting. There is nothing like the rush you get when you are on that stage, when people are interacting with you, when the audience is going to the back to buy your program, when you become a role model that others are inspired by and look up to.

Well that's how I feel about it anyway, that could be biased due to my innate weakness of communicating with people, but I've heard others, even extroverts share the same sentiment. There is nothing like the rush you get from being the speaker. Maybe you could produce your own events and be a promoter, maybe you could be both like what I have done.

The skills that I will cover now will help you with anything you want to do in the speaking world. Online speaking, offline speaking, producing events, marketing events (more in my marketing book than in this one), creating a presentation that converts, the speaking business model and all the ins and outs. This is the guide I wish I had from a younger age to prepare me on how to do this. Most don't even see this as a possible career, they don't even entertain it. I think almost everyone at some point entertains or can see how starting a business could work for them, but it's basically the opposite for speaking, very few ever truly believe they could be the one on the stage.

And thus, they are forever the one looking at the stage.

That is totally fine, and I think we should always be forever learning, but you can learn and you can be the teacher at the same time.

You can admire the stage, but you can still admire it whilst allowing yourself to step on it and command it at the same time. You can shrink from the moment and allow your self doubt to win or you can perform in the face of self doubt and be willing to lose, embarrass yourself and look like a fool (and you may just find you win anyway).

The stage is set, the stage is yours, now it's your turn to decide, will you take it or will you let it go to the next person?

9

The Magician Reveals His Tricks

There are five core components to platform speaking.

1. The audience
2. The business model
3. The offer
4. The presentation
5. The fulfillment

We won't be covering fulfillment in this book. Fulfillment just means how are you delivering what you offered during the presentation. This is something you should, as the expert and business owner, already have a handle on but you will need to adjust your delivery as you start taking on more clients. For example when I offer my "done for you marketing" package on stage then my fulfillment consists of onboarding calls, strategy calls, group calls, then I need a team to assist in creating funnels, ads, customer service and put it all together. The more complex the offer, the harder the fulfillment is. Most speakers generally offer a premium event as the main sale. If you can have group fulfillment that is the easiest and most recommended option to go with.

I will break this down into the three roles for this business model. You have the speaker, which at a bare minimum should be the role you take. You have the promoter, which is the person organizing the event and the schedule. Finally you have the marketer, which is the person filling up the events with the right people for you to speak to - either through advertising or organic invitations. I don't recommend you being all three of these, like I said I don't know anyone else who is all three other than myself, it's a lot to take on especially if you are not tech savvy for the marketing side of things. I do recommend being both the speaker & the promoter.

We will begin with you as the promoter as you need to understand the business model first, and end with you as the speaker as that will be the most in-depth section.

10

Produce Events Like A Pro

Before we can get to the speaking skills, we have to start with the business model and how this industry works. Not many people comprehend or understand how the events industry works as a platform speaker. Note: you do not make money from selling tickets, selling tickets to events does not make you rich and in most instances does not cover the costs of advertising. You make money by selling at the event.

This next section is based on you running your own events, you producing your own events and you setting your own schedule. It will teach you how to think about the industry, what numbers to track and what business model you want to consider.

Let's begin with The Audience

The audience is the most important element to this actually working. No audience, no event, no presentation. Similarly, wrong audience, bad event, lose money and then it turns out to not be viable for you. The audience is also the most difficult part of the whole process as well. You need to literally get people who have never heard of you to turn up to your event and stay hours or even a whole day. People are busy, why should they invest their time into you?

This is what I built a name for myself with, filling up rooms with the right audience. This is what clients hire me to do and this is what I do for myself. I practice what I preach. If you look at any of the photos of my events, and you'll see some with huge audiences, they all were marketed by me, they were all filled by me. The room doesn't fill up on its own or by accident.

When considering the audience the first thing to be aware of is are they a cold or warm audience? A cold audience is an audience that does not know who you are, a warm audience has some idea who you are. The best marketers can fill up rooms with a cold audience, and the best speakers can close to a cold audience. Anyone can sell to a warm audience and ask them to come to an event, but you will have less numbers. Cold audiences are much more scalable, warm audiences are limited by who you know and who knows you. You want to perfect the art of acquiring and closing cold audiences for true mastery in this field.

The next thing to consider is how are you getting the audience to attend?

What I mean by that is are you producing the event yourself and therefore you need to advertise or are you being invited to speak by a promoter?

There's no harm in doing a mixture of both of these you'll just need to be aware of what to look for. Running your events means you are responsible for everything. You need to market and advertise the event to get the audience there. It also means you pay for marketing and advertising and any other costs of the event. You can set your own schedule and you can make as many or as little events that you like, in any location, city, online or offline that you choose. It is completely your own rules. This is what I recommend.

It may sound more daunting because there are more costs, but the benefits far outweigh the costs. The benefit being you keep all the sales and the audience gets to know you instead of other speakers or other events. It will be your name on the event instead of a promoter. Your brand will be built, not theirs.

If the promoter is running the event it means you do not take on any responsibility of advertising, marketing or any of that sort of thing. You just turn up, speak and sell. The promoter pays for all the costs and all the marketing, they get the audience to attend. But beware, this means you will need to give a large percentage of your sales to the promoter. Usually 50%.

There are times when it would make sense to do an event for a promoter. Consider if a promoter flies out a celebrity that costs $200,000 to give a presentation and they are using this celebrity as the draw card. Now that expense is going to justify, in most cases, you not having to pay for anything and instead giving up half of your sales for the opportunity to sell to a much bigger and different audience to what you would be used to selling to. This reduces your cost to basically zero, removes your risk, and gives you a free hit at seeing how well you close.

You need to consider if it is feasible to give away half of your sales. What is the cost of fulfillment? Do you have a backend sale? We will cover that in the business model portion. You also need to be aware that some promoters take a while to pay out. I have heard horror stories about promoters taking 6-18 months to even pay out the sales that you made. Can your business stay afloat for that long if it comes to it? When I invite others to speak at my event I usually pay out in 14-28 days which is a much more reasonable time frame. Review the contracts carefully if you are going to speak at a promoter event.

The other thing I consider when being asked to speak at someone else's event is will I cannibalize my own audience? I.e. They have a celebrity guest speaker that I would like to use in the future. Am I just giving half away when I could have actually just done my own event and kept all of it? Are some or even most of this audience likely to come to my own events where I do not have to give half of my sales away? Especially because my offer is not like most speakers where they have a million upsells, I need to be profitable on the front end to make it worthwhile.

To clarify, my recommendation is to focus on cold audiences and create events that you control. That should make up at least 70% of the events you do. The occasional promoter event can be a part of your schedule here and there only if it makes sense to do so.

What to watch out for if you are invited to speak at another event

If you are invited to speak for an event produced by another promoter, here is your cheat sheet of what to look out for and what to negotiate:

1.

At most you should be prepared to give 50% of the sale price to the promoter. I wouldn't give any more than that.

2.

Are they only taking a percentage of the front end 'first sale' or also your second sale, or is it the lifetime of those customers? You need to make your own decision about what you're willing to accept here. If the event has a massive celebrity that you wouldn't be able to get on your own or they are just too expensive to get on your own, then I would advise being more lenient to giving a percentage of the backend sale as well as the front end. Some big promoters will take 50% of both frontend and backend, I'd aim to try to keep the backend percentage to 30% and avoid lifetime deals unless you don't have a massive ascension model in that case it really wouldn't matter too much for you anyway.

3.

What is the structure of the event? Ideally you don't want to be one in a lineup of seven people all selling at the event. I try to keep my events to a max of two people selling and one keynote with no sale. Are there any speakers that are competitors to you? If there are, you want to speak before them. Speaking earlier in the day is better, or just before the main speaker is also ok if the audience knows the time of when the main speaker will be on.

4.

You need to make sure that you get paid out within 30 days. Some of the promoters will try to keep your money for 6 months or more, have clear dates in the contract and aim for 30 days.

5.

Who collects the sales? Usually the promoter will collect the sales. I prefer this so you don't need to bring staff or payment terminals. Whoever collects should split the sale 50/50 only AFTER 3% fees are taken out for merchant/credit card fees.

6.

What happens in the case of a chargeback or refund? This should be stipulated in the contract. Ideally both are covered by each party equally at least up until a certain time. So for example if you have a 30 day money back guarantee then obviously you would return the money if the refund is requested within 30 days. If the promoter decides to give a refund after the 30 days then that should be on them, unless you also agree to it. In the case of a chargeback you should both be equally responsible.

7.

Are they paying for your expenses? Generally speaking, if you are making a sale at an event, the promoter isn't paying for your flights or accommodation. If they do offer to pay for this, definitely take it as it is not the standard.

8.

Remember that as a new speaker, speaking at someone else's event is the safest way to test out your presentation and offer. There is really no risk or cost for you if you are new. When you become more experienced you may no longer want to entertain promoter events because giving up 50% of sales may be too much for you.

9.

Lastly, consider the audience. Is this audience one you could get on your own? If so you may be giving away 50% of your sales for no reason. Consider would it be possible to just run this event on your own and take the expenses on yourself to keep 100%?

What to watch out for if you are inviting another platform speaker to speak at your event & organizing celebrity events

Let's flip it, now let's cover what to do if you are the promoter/producer and you want someone else to speak at your event. Similar to my Adapt Or Die tour.

1.

If you are aiming for a bigger more qualified audience then you will need to get a drawcard such as a celebrity speaker. There isn't much point inviting another platform speaker to speak at a small event with no drawcard as there will not be a sizable enough audience for you both to sell to. You want to have at least 300 people to justify having multiple platform speakers. If you have 500+ you could even have three, it's totally up to you. Like I said I prefer to keep my events myself, one other platform speaker and a celebrity keynote who does not sell anything

2.

Choosing the celebrity: Each celebrity will have a different price point, so obviously stick to your budget of what you are comfortable with as a first rule. You want to consider what type of person the celebrity will attract? I believe that this is actually more important than the budget rule. If you save maybe $5,000 or $10,000 but you attract the wrong audience then your sales will be worse. If your sale price is $5,000 then really that is only one or two extra sales that you need to make to justify the additional cost of perhaps the better fit for what you have to offer. If you want a business audience then choose a business speaker, like when I did with Mark Bouris. If you want a marketing audience maybe you would go for Gary V. You find the right fit for you. Using a celebrity has a few benefits: it reduces the cost per lead when you run ads, it is more attractive to more people so you will get more sign ups, it will improve your show up rate, it will attract the right audience for you. For any celebrity you are considering, ask yourself how they shape up to those components. If the celebrity is a strong thought leader and has a fanatical following you need to be careful because sometimes that fanatical following isn't great for other speakers. For example when we had Seth Godin as our speaker, a lot of his audience were even offended that anyone else but Seth was speaking on the day, and were even making nasty comments to one of the speakers saying he doesn't align to Seth's values. On the other hand when we had Eric Thomas, the audience was all extremely positive and into personal development so they didn't mind who was speaking they just wanted more. Both had fanatical followings but one of them may not have been the most welcoming for every speaker there. Remember the celebrity isn't the only valuable speaker on the day, you are also valuable. Yes, the crowd is signing up to see them, but this is a perfect example of 'sell them what they want' (they want to hear the celebrity) but give them what they need (they need your knowledge and advice too). The celebrities will also say that they don't want anyone thinking that in the one hour that the celebrity speaks that the audience will have the magic formula to make all their dreams come true. That's not how it works. If the audience really wanted to just see the celebrity they could go on Youtube or buy their book or watch a podcast of them, why come to a whole event if they just wanted to see one person that they could get online for free whenever they wanted? Trust in your own value and make them see that they need you just as much if not more than what they think they need the celebrity.

3.

Is it in person or online? If it is in person then the celebrity will cost more and you will need to pay travel expenses on top. If it is online then it will be cheaper. I advise that only when you are confident and have proven you can sell, is when you go in person. In person costs you more, but you will close at a much higher rate. It is much easier to sell in person than it is online. An online event should always be free and an in person event with a celebrity you can make it paid. If you are doing online you can easily work out the value of the celebrity. I work it out mathematically. For example, if I usually get $20 cost per lead for a free event with only me, and now with the celebrity I am getting $10 cost per lead, then I save $10 for every lead that signs up. How many leads will I need to pay off the cost of the celebrity? Well if they cost $10,000, I essentially need 1,000 sign ups to justify the cost. Anything over 1,000 signups means I am up overall and am maximizing the celebrity. Note: the celebrity should only be paid a fixed fee, not a cut of your sales. If you are the producer of the event no one should get a cut of your sales.

4.

Contacting the celebrity. You won't speak to them directly, you will go through a Speaker Bureau. You can simply Google 'hire (celebrity name) to speak' and see what comes up, you will find speaker bureau's that represent the speaker or they may have an agent that you can contact directly. It's not hard at all to locate these people and communicate with them, it takes some resourcefulness that's all.

5.

Negotiating with the celebrity. You won't really be able to get them to budge on price most of the time, but you can try to include other benefits. I always like to try to include a marketing video from a celebrity that I can use as an ad. Mark Bouris did a great video for the Adapt Or Die tour that we used on the landing page and on the ads. Sometimes you will need to pay more for it, but in my opinion it is worth it because if the audience is a bit skeptical about whether or not the celebrity will actually be there, the video clears those doubts completely. If it is an in person event I also would ask them to take some photos with the VIP ticket holders after the event. Some will say no, some will charge more, make your own decision on this one. I also sometimes buy the books of the speaker and they can generally get you a bulk rate, and I either give this out to the VIPs or I include them in the offer I make at the end, you can also use them as gifts if you prefer. Please plan well in advance if you have no experience with celebrities. It may take a few months to get over the line the first time you work with them.

6.

Choosing the platform speaker. Now that you have the celebrity locked in, it's time to choose who else you want as a platform speaker. You want them to complement you if you are also selling, and you don't want them to be in competition with you. Otherwise you will cannibalize each other's sales. Essentially it should be totally fine and make sense for someone in the audience to invest in you and in your other speaker because the two of you offer different things that may even go hand in hand. If you know them it's even better because then they can reinforce your value and you can also pump them up too. When I chose Aaron for Adapt Or Die, we had already known each other and worked together we knew what each other did, so when he went on stage he told the audience how I run all his ads which gave me a lot of credibility and when I went on I introduced him and gave him the trust the audience had with me. I sold digital marketing and he sold business coaching so they were two different things altogether and it would make sense for someone to want and need both.

7.

Setting the terms with the platform speaker. You should at minimum take 50% of what they sell at your event. The price point of their offer should be at least $4,000. I would also advise asking for 20-30% of the backend too. Most of the bigger promoters actually take 50% of the backend sales, and even collect the sales on the backend as well. This is more than fair because without you the speaker doesn't have the audience. You have had to pay for the whole event on your own. Sometimes if the speaker you invited also has their own events you guys may agree to both only take 50% of the front end for each other so that it is fair for both sides. Up to you though.

8.

In terms of refunds or chargebacks, some as above. Allow the speaker to give a refund within either 14 or 30 days, after that if the speaker decides to give refunds after that date it should be their responsibility and you shouldn't be liable to give back your half. For a chargeback it should be both of you.

9.

Collecting payments. At the event you should take the payments as it is your event, and then you payout within 30 days to the other speaker based on their share. You have expenses to cover for the event, they do not, or if they do they will be very minimal by comparison.

10.

A warning: Lots of these platform speakers are sweet talkers. They will try to make you feel good and say nice sounding things so that they can get what they want. They will even position what they are asking for as if it is a benefit to you, when in reality it is a benefit to them. Never forget that without you there is no event, there is no audience, and you are the one taking the financial risk to pull this off. Do not give them any additional exposure, don't allow them to hijack the event and make it all about themselves, keep your wits about you. You will get asked by many speakers if they can come to speak at your events too. Never let someone you aren't sure about speak at your event. If you are not sure about their ethics, don't do it. If you are not sure that they will be fair and honest with their sales, don't do it. If they have high refund rates, don't do it. Only work with people you trust, and in this industry that is really not many people. You may even find out after you work with them that maybe you shouldn't for the next time.

Further Leveraging Celebrity Events

Organizing and running these larger celebrity events are a great way to create connections with other people that you may have been trying to connect with or that could be a good relationship for you in the future. For example in my story you would have seen how I used my celebrity events to also leverage into other relationships such as in the Eric Thomas event I was able to then reach out to Owen Cook and we now still have a great relationship. In the Seth Godin event that is how I got connected to Aaron Sansoni. Those events also led me onto other referrals. I met Joel Bauer because someone I knew had seen me do an event with Seth and introduced me to Joel. So on and so forth.

Remember some of these events are not only about profit, they are also about power, credibility and positioning. The doors you can open when you create these events go far beyond the event itself. If you have a list of people you looked up to or people you thought would be a great business relationship for you, work out if it makes sense to leverage the event to also connect with them.

A lot of people ask me how do I create connections with a lot of these celebrities or highly successful business owners, and the old cliché is to approach them with value i.e. what are you offering them. That has basically been my strategy, I have never asked them for anything, I have only offered them opportunities that do not normally come up. That style of approach gets you respect, is different to 99% of people that approach them and is low to no risk for them because they are essentially getting free exposure to the audience that you created. You are giving massive value by having them speak at an event with a celebrity, which of course is going to open doors for you to then build that into something else. Everyone else they meet usually asks them for something without giving anything of value first.

11

What To Sell As A Speaker

Before you even think of stepping on a stage and making a presentation, you must understand the business model. You need to understand how to monetise your events. Let's jump into the foundational principles for both online and offline events.

The Model Of Free To Fee

Regardless if your event is online or offline it should be free to attend. The only time you wouldn't make it free is when you have a celebrity in person event. That is the only time. Many egos will get crushed here 'I don't do anything for free', well then you are missing out on getting even better results. It's as simple as that.

It's important to understand that we are only talking about front end events not back end events. The front end just means this is the first time they are seeing you. Think about it, you see some random person online and the ad says come to my seminar about how to improve your business, only $47. You have no idea who they are, they are not a celebrity, you don't recognise anything about the person, are you pulling out your credit card and paying for the event? Heck ask yourself to review your actions over the last 5 years, how many free events have you attended vs how many paid events have you attended that didn't have a celebrity or draw card you knew in advance?

Ok Ethan, but what if my event is so cheap like $20, can I make them pay $20?

No. It doesn't matter if the event is $1. It doesn't matter if it's a refundable deposit just to make them show up. The simple answer is this: if the attendee needs to put their credit card details into your page just to secure their spot, you are going to be wasting your ad money. This is not from a 'feeling' or intuition, this is from having tested all of this over and over again. The increase in cost per attendee is 3-5x more, sometimes even 10x. Keep your event free. Even Grant Cardone is now using free events to get new leads. I've seen 5 day events with celebrities such as Floyd Mayweather, Snoop Dogg and Magic Johnson be completely FREE to attend. You need more volume, don't worry about having them pay to attend, your numbers will be much smaller.

If your idea was to make them pay because you think it will be profitable before the event even starts, then you have another thing coming. The $47 you want to charge for a ticket will still be acquired at a loss. It may cost you $100-200 just to sell one $47 ticket. There is simply no point in trying to go to a cold audience and ask for money straight out of the gate, it's also quite rude and abrupt.

Imagine if you were walking down the street, and some random person jumps out at you and says "Hey you don't know me but do you want to buy this new skin cream for $50?" You're probably going to be confused and just walk by feeling like that guy was just a used car salesman. So if you wouldn't do that in real life, why would you do the digital equivalent of that online?

Take the ego out of it, it doesn't 'cheapen' anything, it makes it more accessible, it reduces friction. I want you to remember that, it's about the friction. It's about being customer centric. You are showing that you respect the customer because you are emotionally intelligent enough to realize that they are already giving you their most important asset, their time, and they don't even know who you are, don't make them get out their credit card too. Our brains are lazy, it takes a lot of proof and convincing for us to even believe that it is worth our time to attend something let alone pay for something we aren't sure about and then attend. Be customer centric. A credit card is friction, a payment is friction, even turning up to the event is friction, finding parking, taking a day out of your schedule it's all friction. Removing the credit card up front removes the friction from the beginning. Which means more people will get through the funnel, we need volume!

Online Vs Offline Events

I believe you should do both. You'll attract different people and you'll learn different skills. In the online event space you don't need fancy equipment, I just do my events off my computer webcam and no other microphone. You don't need equipment. I also like online events because I can get away with wearing a hoodie and more casual clothes.

Online events will cost much less. There are no travel costs, no hotel costs, no AV and all of that. As a beginner it is a great way to test your presentation and get really good at it for a much lower cost. On the other hand with offline events you need to factor in the additional costs. Finding a decent venue at a decent hotel (like Marriott, Hilton) plus the AV costs are going to set you back at least $3k-5k. Not to mention if you are traveling as well. For in person events after all these costs and the ad spend I would set aside at least $10,000 per event. For online events you may just have a $3,000 bill for ads, that's it.

Please also do not feel like you need to pay for coffee and tea or food at a free event. I can't believe how rude some people are, and they will say oh wow there's no coffee or food, you mean I have to pay for that? You are producing a free event off your own dollar, giving so much to this audience for free and some are worried about paying $5 for a coffee or $50 for parking, are you serious?! Ignore these people, they are the exception not the rule. Do not pay for coffee and food. It will set you back so much more and it is not industry standard to do that. What I love about Singapore & Malaysia though is that they will actually include coffee and tea for your event in your room hire fee, they don't charge you any extra to provide it to your guests.

The plus side to in person events though is that you will sell better. Your closing rates will increase. You can also charge more. So you charge more, and your closing rates go up which is why the in person events are usually more profitable.

An in person event can be anywhere from 4 hours up to a full day. I see some people doing multi day free events, I just think that's overkill and there's no need. If you are good at closing you can close in 4-8 hours at high ticket prices. An online event generally is two hours, however you could do a multi day event here: 2-3 hours per day over 3 days is a format that does work online. Personally I stick to my first online event as 2 hours (very rarely I will do a 5 hour online event as my first step) and in person I will do 4-8 hours.

You want to choose the length of the event based on what you are selling and what the price point is. The more time the audience spends with you the more they trust you and the more they understand your process and how credible you are. At the same time though, the longer the event goes, the higher the chance they may need to leave and miss your offer altogether! By credibility I don't mean by showing awards and testimonials, the way you speak about things conveys credibility much more than anything else. If you are selling higher ticket priced programs you need more time. For example, at an online event I sell a $5,000 program in 2 hours, you may need 4 hours to do that. At the same time I have sold at $10,000 and $25,000 within 2 hours online too, but they are the exception and not the rule. If your price point is only $497 or $997 you only need an hour or 90 minutes maximum.

If you have multiple offers then you will need more time as well. When I have three offers I spend at least two hours for online events and four hours in person.

You also want to consider where geographically you will do your events. For in person events you may actually find that you close better when you go internationally. For online events, I have always found you do better locally, which makes sense, people are more skeptical online. In person they can verify that you are real so to speak. Start online events in your local country and then once you start to become profitable try to do some in person events and see if your success transfers over to the online world. I did it the opposite way, I started in person and then was forced to go online. You need a higher appetite for risk and a thick skin if you want to start in person because you might be down $10,000 after the first event like I was.

The last difference is the interaction. This is really everything when it comes to events. Now in person you obviously get the verbal and physical interaction. Whether it is raising hands or it is a verbal yes, or even live coaching and demonstrations. But, you need to be ready for anything and you need to be able to command a stage. If someone talks out during your seminar, are you able to handle it? If someone gets too loud, can you take control back of the room? If someone asks a hard question can you navigate it so that you don't lose the entire room? You have to be really strong in your frame, because you can get hit with anything.

With online events, sure you don't have the atmosphere and the physical feedback like you do in person. It is much more difficult to get someone to focus because they are watching you on their own on a small computer screen, they don't have the environment of everyone else around them, so I would argue that you actually need to be a better speaker in some ways to do well online. Most people simply don't have the attention span to watch anything other than Netflix for over an hour. What I love about online that you don't get in person, is the chat box. There's something very exciting about seeing 100 messages all come through at once, everyone is responding and participating. Even shy people like myself, it's easier for anyone to interact online whereas in person usually the more confident people will participate more often. You need a lot more interaction online to keep everyone engaged, and we will go through how to do that later on.

The Sales Process Of Online & Offline Events

We will talk about how to sell and close in the section about you as a speaker, before that though you need to have the plan on the actual sales process. Let's start with the online sales process first.

Scenario #1: You have one offer only

I do advise that you have one offer. Especially as a beginner when so much can go wrong in the close, having one offer guarantees that it will be simple. Whereas when you have multiple offers it can be confusing for the audience. If you are going to have multiple offers they need to be vastly different from each other. They can't be "kinda" different. For example if your first offer is 8 weeks of group coaching, your second offer cannot be 12 weeks of group coaching - it's just way too similar. The brain makes decisions based on differences, they need to be substantial, otherwise we get confused and we end up not buying anything.

When you are on a promoter's stage, you can only have one offer anyway. Best to practice from the start with mastering your sale of one option. If you have a backend event, by all means offer multiple things for sure, but in a 2 hour online event best to stick to one.

Firstly with online you don't have signup forms and payment terminals so you need to prepare an online payment link in advance. You can use Stripe's internal payment page or you can do what I do and make custom sales pages using Clickfunnels. You need to set up this before the event so you can take payment online.

Stripe is a payment gateway, like PayPal, and it connects to Clickfunnels. You can also use PayPal. I just don't like how they treat business owners and have heard too many horror stories, so I avoid it when I can.

Now you base your sales process on the price of your offer. If your offer is less than $2,000, you will instruct the audience to go to the sales page and buy online whilst the seminar is still going. So you make the offer, they click the link and then they go buy with their credit card. You get the link from Clickfunnels, post it in the chat box and have it on the slide as well. The chat box is most important though, that way the audience can click it directly.

You may also choose to have a QR code on your slide. This means the audience can use their phone to buy. Totally optional and up to you if you use the QR for your offer.

If your price is over $2,000 you have decisions to make. Over $2,000 is the threshold of what people are used to paying during an online event. So there are some options you have. If your price point is around $5,000 (which is where I sell at), then you can either drive them to the sales page or you can drive them to a call back form or you can do a combo of both. When you are starting out, I would do a call back form if you have someone that can do the calls. This is because you will close more deals and at the start you need revenue. If you sell at $10,000 or more you almost definitely want to drive them to a booked call. This is a 45-60 minute call that you have a proper discussion with them one on one and they pay on the call. I personally don't love that because the benefit for me with seminars is closing people then and there.

With the $5,000 offer call, the difference is that those calls are only 5-10 minutes long and happen immediately after the seminar is done. You may have a list of five people, you call one at a time and process payments over the phone. You must collect payment with them on the phone, don't get them to go back, hang up the phone and do it in their own time because chances are, it won't happen.

When I started online events I pushed everyone to a call back form, using Google Forms, and we would call them immediately after. This works extremely well. As I got better, I drove people directly to a sales page for $5,000 where they pay online and then I say if you are seriously interested but have a question fill out the form and we will call you right now. This way we had those that didn't need a call pay straight away, and those that did we didn't miss out on them either.

Scenario #2: You have multiple offers

There are some instances where you may want to consider multiple offers. You may have a low ticket offer that you want to provide for people that aren't ready to join your main program, you may also have a high end program that you want to see if you can sell straight away, or you may just want to position your best seller as a complete no brainer. This is a form of price anchoring. I.e. if you want to sell your offer for $5,000, it looks much cheaper compared to a $10,000 offer standing right beside it.

There are some risks though. Some people just want to buy the best of everything, so if your main offer that you want to sell more of is $5,000, but you also have a $15,000 offer that you have mentioned too, that may make the $5,000 offer seem not as valuable and the $15,000 is what I need. If I don't have $15,000 then I will not buy anything. This may seem counterintuitive but there are many people like this.

The other risk is that it is too confusing. If you have different offers, it can be hard to remember what the differences are and what I get in each. They need to be vastly different and you'll need to go slower or tell them which of the options are best for them.

If you are going to do it, I would advise having three options and having your best seller be the middle one price wise (or the highest one, if it is at least $5,000). I split mine up by categories, my first offer is do it yourself, then it is done with you then it is done for you. The price points were $997, $1,997 and $5,000. Most people went for the $5,000 option. This doesn't mean it will be the same for you, it's whatever you push more. For me the $5,000 is the most valuable solution so by making it the most expensive it is also positioned as the best available. It's also not a price point that is too expensive, most people have or can get $5,000. Not everyone will have $15,000. What this also did was give people a chance to get in at any price and upgrade later on. I.e. if they did the $1,997 offer and later on wanted to upgrade, I would honor the price and take it off what they paid.

In this scenario you go through each offer individually without revealing the price first, this way they know all of the options and they can start thinking about which one they want. Then you go over them again in more depth, revealing the price and the link for them to and buy. For the highest price point you can push them to have the instant call with you as now it is a more exclusive option. Those that wanted the lower price options have already gone and paid, those that wanted the higher price have now put their details down, and you call them straight away and you tell them to expect a call straight away. If there are lots of people on the form then you should text them to tell them it may be a 30 minute wait. Do it on the day whilst it is fresh in their mind, the sooner the better.

The In Person Sales Process

Scenario #1: Table Rush Method - One Offer

This is what you think about when you think of platform speakers. One offer, go to the back of the room, sign up now. This was what I did at Adapt Or Die & what I witnessed the other speakers do my first time seeing this happen live.

Essentially you have one core presentation, one core offer of no more than $5,000 and no less than $3,000 and you have payment forms at the back of the room. I also bring payment terminals to collect the payment right there, some however just ask people to write down their credit card details on the form and then they go and process it on Stripe or any payment gateway manually. The benefits of taking payment there is that if a payment fails you can work it out with the person straight away, it also seems more legitimate as people in stores are used to paying immediately using a payment terminal. They also don't need to write down their credit card details on the sheet of paper if that makes them feel uncomfortable. The benefit of only having the forms and not having them pay with their credit card on the day, is that it is quicker. When you have large volumes of people trying to pay and you only have 5 or 6 terminals, that can create a bit of a line and delay which may lose sales or delay the event. By only having forms it is quicker in real time and can avoid this delay.

You won't need an online payment link for this (although you could as a backup too) but you will need contracts and payment forms for them to sign on the day. Try to keep this as short as possible, ideally one double sided A4. You should have helpers at the sales tables who are in charge of collecting payments. Instruct them to take payments of those that are ready to go first. Anyone that has questions, ask them to go to the side and wait. You need to collect first, and do the rest later. You don't want the heartbreak of spending 45 minutes with one person asking a million questions only to say they have to think about it, and instead you could have been talking to 10 serious people in that time. You need to have at least one person at the sales tables that is confident about the process and understands the offer so they can handle any questions and even help push people over the line.

Once you are finished with your presentation, you can also go back to the sales tables and handle any questions, help out if they need you and just reassure people that are already there buying. Especially if you see many people waiting to be served, it's a good idea to jump in and go mingle. Which

I also did at Adapt or Die and this does help. Again these should be closing conversations, not a 'can I pick your brain' conversation.

The one close offer in person is the classic and it is something you need to have in your arsenal. Realistically you should be able to sell it in 2 hours as that's all you would get on a bigger promoter's stage. If you can get this presentation to close 10% of the audience or more you are doing very well.

This style can be used for any sort of front end event. Remember a front end event is an event where it is the first time they see you and they have not bought anything from you yet.

Scenario #2: Multiple Offers

Unlike online events, where I advise that the program you want to sell be your highest option and be around the $5,000 mark, in person you can charge more. So if you are going to have multiple offers you can even get away with four offers and have a higher priced offer such as a $10-15,000 option and you can find yourself selling a few of these.

You also shouldn't really have a low ticket $997 offer. These could be sold in the half way break if you have one just to cover costs, but do not sell a low ticket item in person during your main close, you are wasting your audience. For example if my in person event was planned to be all day, I may schedule it as the following: 9am start, 12:30pm offer a 497-997 product, one hour lunch break until 2pm, 2pm-5pm content and then at the end make my high ticket offer at the end. 5pm-7pm hold the room until all the sales have been processed. That would be an example schedule if you wanted to make a low ticket offer and have a full day event.

I usually would stick to three offers, at about $3,000, $7,500 and $15,000, however you could go for a fourth offer. The fourth offer is there to act as a decoy to frame the highest option as having even more value. I.e. if $15,000 was your highest offer and what you wanted to sell more of, then by adding a $12,000 offer you make the $15,000 seem less expensive and you should have a lot more value in the $15,000 offer so that by comparison the $15,000 looks incredible value wise.

The sales process for this is a bit different. Here you aren't going to enable a table rush of people going to the back to buy on the spot. Instead you want to have a strategist or sales person with you at this event, and it is their job to close. When you are explaining the offer, you will have your assistant hand out a sales sheet to the audience which will have all of your options that you are going to offer. The price points should be blank on this sheet. Once you are explaining the offer and revealing the price point, the audience writes it in on their sheet. This keeps them engaged. Then when you have finished explaining all of the offers, you instruct the audience to go to the back, where you will have a sheet of paper where they can put their name down and write down what option they want to invest in. Keep in mind you must also make sure that they know the prices are for today only and the offers are for today only.

Then what you do is you have a short break, your strategist may extract all of them from the room and explain what will happen, and then you go back to the room or you have another speaker do that, and it is your job to hold the room. This essentially means you keep speaking until the strategist has completed their one on one sales conversations. Whilst you are speaking the strategist takes those interested out of the room one by one for a conversation and they will collect payments during that conversation. Ideally for this to work you want: higher price points, an assistant to take payments and a strategist to close one on one sales. You'll remember this is the same methodology that was used when I bought the $33,500 coaching program. It is very effective, works great for high ticket and still makes sure you collect payment then and there on the day. You'll just need more content in your arsenal to hold the room at the end.

In terms of any one on one sales conversations, we aren't going to go into that as this book is focused on the speaking element. I cover the one on one sales in my training and coaching.

The Numbers Behind The Platform Speaking Industry Model

In person events

As you are producing your own events you need to also understand the numbers and what to expect. This isn't a model where you can just test a small little budget like $1,000 and expect to see $100,000 back. This isn't an industry for the faint of heart, you might have an event that produces nothing, no sales, no revenue and you will have to wake up in the morning wondering if you give up or if you soldier on. Do not come complaining and whining, there's no room for average in the speaking industry, you've got to be great.

In the speaking industry YOU set the goal first. YOU set the amount of people that you want there and you work backwards. You don't ask 'how much do I need to spend to get x amount of people' that is a broken mentality. You set a goal and say I want 100 people there, let's get that. You need to work backwards to give you any sense of comfort when it comes to the numbers.

Here is how we do that.

First step is what amount of people should you aim for? I personally like 80-120 people for an event that is just me as the main speaker. So think about the events I did with Reggie, with Les, the Rockstar Speaker tour and even the Sold Out Seminars tour. I want 80-120 in attendance when it comes to an in person event.

My next step is to go find the right venue. If our aim is for 80-120 people, I am finding a room that only fits 70-100. Why is that? Because most of these venues dramatically underestimate their room size. There was one room they told us would fit 150 and we fit 250 for example. It's not to save costs, it's to give it that atmosphere that is so hard to find. A smaller room gives you more atmosphere. And more atmosphere gives you everything, the adrenaline rush, the buzz, the sales, all happen from the atmosphere. Book the smaller room, get the extra chairs and you will make it fit. And if not, there's always standing room. Of course you should check with the hotel first, as some really do have tiny spaces. You don't want a tiny space, you want a room that actually fits 100 people, not 200. Otherwise it feels so empty. We had one location that said they could fit 80. That for me was probably the tightest room we have had, we managed to fit 120 and had some standing room too. Also people leave after lunch break so you want to keep the full room energy.

For the room you should anticipate about a $3,000 fee for the whole day and you may also need to pay an additional $1,000-2,000 for AV. The AV you will need is a projector, microphones for the speaker, I prefer the headset but most will have lapel, (perhaps one roaming for the audience) and audio. So $5,000 for the venue alone. If you are staying at the hotel try to get discounted rates on everything else you do there and sign up to any loyalty programs.

Then it's time to work backwards on the amount of people you want to attend. Let's say you want 100 people in attendance. With in person events you want to plan for a 20% show up rate. It might be higher it might be lower, if you can get 20% show up you are around the industry standard or even slightly above it. So that means we need 500 people to get 100 to show up. To get one person to register it can cost anywhere between $10-$100 depending on your niche, industry, country you are targeting, target market, marketing skills and marketing angles. On average you want to aim for no higher than $20 per registration. If you are targeting Malaysia for example you can get signups for a couple of dollars. Usually Australia, USA, Canada are more expensive, Asia is cheaper. Europe can also be a bit pricey. If you get $20 cost per sign up and 20% show up, we are looking at $100 per show up and $10,000 in total ad spend. It is possible to get $10 per registration and we generally get $10-15 but I'd rather work on worst case numbers than best case numbers.

The bigger cities are usually cheaper, the smaller cities more expensive when it comes to advertising, this is the opposite for when it comes to room and venue hire. Choose which cities you will go to, I like to choose those close in proximity and I do three at a time, I.e. Brisbane, Melbourne & Sydney. Space them out as you wish, for one day events you can do them back to back or if you would like to have a small holiday in one of the cities take a few extra days.

Now you might be thinking well hang on, $10,000 is a lot. Well then you can do an event for 50 people and budget $5,000 instead when you are starting out. You don't have to have 80-120, aim for a lower number for your first try. Then shift your belief around how much $10,000 actually is. If you price your products the way I have mentioned above, then you should only need one or two sales to cover the $10,000. Which leads me to my next set of numbers: the closing percentage.

In the above scenario we are getting $100 per person to show up to the event. This is a very profitable number. If you can consistently get $100 per attendee you should be very profitable. Why is that? Because of the way you close at the event.

In person you should be able to close 10%. Let's say you have a kind of low price point of $3,000. If you close 10% of a room full of 100 people that is 10x$3,000 = $30,000. And usually for speakers they also have another sale after the first sale. That one would basically be all profit.

Let's say you had a more recommended price point of $5,000. You would make $50,000 in sales from a room of 100 people closing at 10%. So if you spend $10,000 on ads, $5,000 on the venue, $50,000-$15,000 = $35,000 in profit from one days work. Not bad.

The issues arise when you only spend $1,000. Because even if you hit your KPI of $100 per show up, ten people at an event isn't exactly going to give you a great atmosphere or energy and if it's your first time this may mean you bomb out and think that you can't hack it or that something didn't work. Dedicate the proper amount to making this work.

The beauty about this industry too is even if you screw up and get $200 per attendee, if you still close 10% you are still very profitable.

Online Events

The great thing with online events is that instantly your AV and venue hire costs go to zero. You literally don't need anything other than your computer. You don't need to go and buy a microphone, you don't need a fancy camera or any other equipment, you can do this on your laptop. You don't even need to dress up for the online events.

What made my style very different to how most people run online events is that I started by acting in the same exact way as if it were an in person event when it came to choosing locations. I would still do one city at a time. Eventually I expanded this to one timezone at a time. I still advise when starting out to do one city at a time because if you do want to go in person you have a list and when they come to the online event you can speak directly about their city and that is a bonding tie that all of the attendees have when they come to your event.

In terms of cost per lead, they are pretty similar to the in person cost per lead, if anything slightly cheaper. I aim for under $20 cost per lead. So we are still looking at trying to stay under or around the $100 cost per attendee. The other difference is that you will most likely have a reduced closing percentage. There is no social proof online, well there is but it isn't the same as seeing everyone around get up to go to the back of the room. Naturally you won't close at the same percentage for the same price point. I still aim for 10%, 10% online is world class when closing to a cold audience. Of course a warm audience could be anything and the price point changes this number too, but if you can close 10% of a cold audience at a price point of over $3,000 that is world class numbers. In reality you should aim for 5-8%. Still very profitable.

Let's take $10,000 spent on ads, 100 people there, close 5% of 100 at $5,000 = $25,000 in sales, you have made $15,000 profit in the one event. Then add in the up sell and you are well ahead. Of course, you can hit these numbers with much less spent in ads, we have had events where we spend $3,000 and end up converting that into $40,000 in sales. I want you to work with worst case numbers so that you see even if you only get $100 cost per show up, you will be very profitable if you can close properly.

Understanding Variables

Running events all comes down to variables. If you have a statistical or mathematical background you're most likely very used to the term. A variable is essentially an element to the equation that contributes to the end result. In the event industry the main variables are cost per lead, cost per show up rate, show up rate percentage and closing rate percentage. If you have a poor event or a result that wasn't what you expected you need to look at it mathematically and logically, not emotionally and hysterically. Assess which variable was the issue and then address the bottleneck. The bottleneck is just the area of the event that caused the failure of the event.

For example if you had spent $10,000 on ads, only had 1 sale, 20 people showed up and 500 people registered. Your bottleneck isn't that you only closed one out of 20, your bottleneck was not your cost per lead (you still had $20 cost per lead), your bottleneck was that less than 5% of registrations actually turned up! Your cost per show up was $500 instead of the $100 we aim for. Then we can assess that and we can say ok well why did so few show up? Was there no incentive? Did we remind them? Did the emails go out, did we text them, did we call them? What did we do differently or out of the ordinary? Was there a public event on, that we didn't know about, was today a holiday or religious day?

A variable could be a name change. Maybe you have done the same event and it's worked well, but then you change the name to try something new and it actually backfired. That's also a variable. Something as simple as a word on an ad or a text with the location in it versus with no location can make all the difference. The speakers are a variable too, the time of the event is a variable, the offer is a variable. Track absolutely everything and keep a spreadsheet of what you have changed and when.

This is also the same process for when you have a very good result too. You want to work backwards and understand why it worked so well.

The key to look out for are any outliers. An outlier is a variable that is so far out of the norm that you need to disqualify it. For example, when my first event was during a snowstorm, that is an outlier. Which makes the whole event an outlier. Which means logically I need to separate my emotions for my actions and disqualify that event altogether from my decision making. Regardless of how much money and time I have lost. You can't control outliers.

The event business is all about numbers, variables and outliers. Assess all of them before, during and after the event and you will find your areas for improvement and optimisation.

A Word Of Caution

Before we move onto perhaps the most important model and numbers behind these models, I want to give you one final word of caution about this industry. When I entered it I thought all the speakers must be incredible people that wanted to make the world a better place, that they would be completely out of my league and I would have to do my best to make a mark and create an impact. However after about a year of speaking and once I started meeting a lot of the speakers, I quickly realized that perhaps this may not be true.

In fact I am saddened to say that this industry is rife with poor behavior, unethical behavior and just straight out fake behavior too. This is an industry where image means more than providing a great service, money means more than relationships and reputation means more than character. In fact it's actually extremely difficult to find platform speakers that have good intentions for at least 90% of their actions.

I am not going to name names, there's no point, the dodgy speakers know who they are. Some of them probably don't even think they are dodgy, that's how self absorbed they are, but alas, hopefully the marketplace is smart enough to realize. It is a very self absorbed industry, you have to have a little bit of an ego to pull this off, no doubt, but there are levels to it.

I have never seen an industry where it is so common for people to just fake their numbers. They blatantly lie to their audiences. Not just by a little bit, no, by a lot. All kinds of numbers such as how much they make, how many people attended their events, how many clients they have, how much money their clients have made, and much more. It really dismayed me to see some of the issues, but I realized I have to try to be one of the few that can change the industry from the inside.

One of the obvious things to look out for is when someone says they have 'shared the stage' with someone else. Usually this is just bullshit. Ok there's a difference between organizing an event with a celebrity speaker and simply being invited to do a 90 minute presentation on the same day. When you are organizing it, doing a Q&A with them, that is sharing the stage, that is working with the celebrity. But what most of these speakers do, is they fool you with these nice sounding words like "I shared the stage with Gary V" when in reality all they did was speak for 90 minutes, because the promoter needed someone to sell so they make money, and Gary V doesn't know them from a bar of soap.

Most speakers are like this in this industry unfortunately.

The next thing to keep in mind, is that they usually have a million and one upsells to sell you. I'm not saying that is a bad thing, and every business needs opportunities to upsell and cross sell, however there comes a point where it's just lunacy. More than that, when speakers promise you the world when you buy their $3,000 program, but in reality you only get all of those things when you buy into their $40,000+ program. There's no transparency there, and there is very little authenticity either. Hence why they get so many complaints from customers.

The last part is that most speakers just pump your state full of good emotions. Actually sit down and listen to one of these people speak, are they just getting the crowd emotionally engaged and priming them to buy or is their content actually dense and useful? 90% of speakers are emotional masters. The whole event is designed to get you primed to buy, have you emotionally ready to buy and then buy again, so that you walk out feeling like wow what an amazing event and so that you spend everything that they ask for. There is a fine balance required between the two elements, yes it needs to be a great event, yes you should do what you can to make sales but above all it has to be ethical.

I've even seen this behavior at different paid events from various speakers from all over the world. Literally people have paid over $3,000 for this event and the whole thing is pretty much 10% content, 90% prime you to buy again. It's so unethical, yet the attendees aren't even aware. I wasn't aware when I was the one attending these events at the beginning of my journey too. People buy emotionally and so some speakers absolutely capitalize on this.

I tell you this though, when I see people come to us in tears because they have just dropped $40,000-100,000+ with someone else and have gotten zero results, it says everything I need to know. No amount of nice emotions can help someone when they have just given away everything, but that's what a lot of speakers rely on, and it gives a terrible name to the industry.

In fact one of the issues I faced when starting was I thought that you had to be that type of speaker that just pumps everyone up. No, you don't. In fact, please don't be like that. Funnily enough, it's usually the speakers that have studied and proudly display their NLP credentials that are like this.

It's not that I am against NLP, it's that I asked one of the senior people when I worked at Neuro-Insight about it, and even they said it's not grounded in any neuroscience. NLP when used by the wrong person is an absolute disaster. Anyway, you don't need NLP and rah-rah jumping up and down to do this, and if a speaker does it, I run away. You need to be an expert at using language instead of 'tactics' with NLP to be a great speaker, and Joel Bauer is an expert at language. I've felt my speaker delivery and the words I say whilst on stage, even the way I phrase and structure sentences have been greatly improved by listening to him.

So please watch out for these types of speakers. Although me and JT Foxx have had our differences, I greatly respect that he is also a straight shooter, he doesn't care if you feel good or bad after the seminar he will tell it to you straight. Now do I agree with the way he does some things, how he sells or what he offers as his main sale? No I don't. But that's ok and we can have different opinions, that's healthy. He was the first speaker I properly got to analyze, and I think that watching his delivery greatly allowed me to step into a similar style of straight forward no wishy washy stuff, which I am very grateful for. He also had incredible coaches, whereas other speakers just use their past clients who usually don't even have more success or credentials than the person they are coaching, and are not equipped to deliver what a real coach should be able to.

Overall this industry is like a minefield, be careful where you step and be aware most of what people are selling is not what it seems, most of them just want you to feel good so you buy (these are in my opinion the worst type of speakers), they leave customers really hurt financially and you never find out because they manage them to make the customer feel good again so that they don't leave a bad review. These customers then never trust anyone else because of how they were treated.

It's hard to tread the minefield, because the speakers are so good at bullshitting to your face. When you make it in this industry, do right by the people, put your ethics and morals before the dollar and maybe together we can start to slowly change it. That's my mentality now, I have to get to the audience first because if they buy from these other people they may be forever scarred and perhaps never even end up starting that business or chasing that dream. Be careful and keep your wits about you as both a speaker and also a consumer.

A Warning About Some of The Ads You See Online

The last warning you need to be aware of is about the ads you see online. There has been this growing trend of experts trying to tell you that you don't need a funnel, or webinar, or Facebook ads to be successful. Some even say that funnels don't work and all of this crap. Essentially you need to be smarter than to fall for this. What they are doing is trying to position themselves as different to anything else. However if you pay attention, you'll notice they tell you not to do one thing, then proceed to do the exact thing they tell you not to do. It's completely incongruent and hypocritical, I'm always stunned how people fall for that.

Every ad is a funnel. So by definition if the ad is telling you not to do funnels or not to do ads they are lying straight to your face. The people saying this are only doing so for attention and because they don't actually know what works. The truth is every single online business has a funnel, all types of funnels can work, all types of ads can work, it's just what is going to work best for your business and your lifestyle that you choose.

Don't listen to these people trying to tell you ads and funnels don't work anymore; they have no idea what they are talking about and usually are the ones with the most complex funnels anyway!

The Business Model

The final important aspect before we dive into understanding how to create presentations that convert, is understanding your business model.

Like any business, you don't want to have a transactional business. A transactional business essentially means that a customer buys once from you and never buys again. If you look at the vast majority of most successful businesses in the world, and most successful speakers in the world, they have upsells and cross sells. They create a relationship based or a recurring business. Without a good business model you are leaving money on the table which puts more strain on you as the speaker to perform exceptionally well every single time.

A phrase that you may be aware of when referring to a longer term business model is an ascension model or a value ladder. All that means is what are the steps in your funnel that a customer can go to and from. For example with my value ladder it is as simple as the following:

Step 1:

First contact with a prospect is when they come to my free seminar (or low cost seminar if a celebrity event)

Step 2:

I can then offer either 1. Done For You Marketing $5,000 or 2. An educational seminar for 3 or 4 days for $3-5,000.

Step 3:

From there if they buy the education seminar I can offer either ongoing marketing services (monthly recurring payments) or one on one or group coaching ($30,000+). If they buy the done for you program they can ascend into a monthly retainer from there.

Now why is this so important? Let's sub in some of the numbers we mentioned before.

If we get $100 per show up and we have 100 people attend our event, we would have spent $10,000 on ads and $5,000 on the venue so that is $15,000 in costs and let's say we close 10% at $5,000, we make $50,000 revenue. Which is a total of $35,000 in profit. That's great but what if one day we have an off day and our profit is only $15,000 or $10,000? If you only have one offer, you put strain on your model to always be successful on the front end.

Now let's say for every ten people that buy, two of them stay on for $3,000 per month for a year. So that's two people paying $36,000 per year = $72,000. Now we have turned that $35,000 or $15,000 profit into $72,000. Now you have more budget to spend on ads, you can use that to get more people to attend, because you KNOW your numbers. If I know 10% close on front end and 20% close on backend I can be sure of myself to spend the right amount and to scale to the right spot. Who wouldn't spend $15,000 total to make over $100,000 in revenue? You'd do it again and again. That revenue number becomes a lot bigger when you get a proper backend.

This doesn't mean stop everything until you work out what you are going to sell after the main sale, no. You should perfect your first sell and your first offer first otherwise you won't have anyone to make an offer to on the backend anyway. Your first offer is much more important, much harder to get right and requires a lot more skill. Once they experience you it is much more likely they will buy again from you.

Here is a little secret, most of my biggest and best clients are actually totally happy to only breakeven on the front end or even lose money. Yes, that's correct. Why is that? Because all the money for them is in the backend.

My model is an exception to the norm. Most speakers do not offer done for you services, it's too much work for too little price. They offer education only instead. Much higher profits, less work, all finished after a 3 or 4 day event. When I came into the market as a speaker, I was of the impression that all of these speakers with all of their upsells are ripping people off and I can offer a better service for a tenth of what they were offering. Literally they were offering $30,000+ to just tell people what to do, I was offering $5,000 to actually do it for you.

As I got more experience I realized why they did the upsell. Yes some of them, I still think most of them, are really offering minimal value for what they charge, I do still believe that, but I can now understand why it is done and how it does change the game business wise. However what most of them do, is have a hard sell and they really push. My upsell is so lowkey I don't even offer it to everyone. It's a case by case basis. Which is where I differ dramatically, you won't be pushed to spend $30-80,000 with me, yet others will do that for much less value than what you would get from me for

$5-15k. Seriously, you have people paying heaps of money just to be told by someone what to do like they are some sort of messiah. Then they have no money for ads and wonder why they aren't successful. Anyway, I digress.

You need to have an upsell but you need to not be dodgy about it. Actually offer something that will help people get a better result. That is the point of the upsell. It is to help people get a better result, by getting more access to you. How to think about the ascension model is that the more expensive it is, the more access they get to you.

Let's take a more traditional platform speaker model:

They run ads to a free event and they offer a $497-997 three or four day event. This will mean they break even or lose money on their ads. Most people can't comprehend that and stress out when they don't double their money. The best in the business revenue wise, lose on the front end. If $100 per show up, and you close 10% you are breaking even selling $997. They spend lots more on ads, just want volume, because they know they will close at their own event in the next step.

Let's say they spend $50,000 on ads. They have 500 people show up. Let's say they close 100 people at $497. A higher conversion rate because it is such a low price.

At the 3-4 day event lets say they close 20% of the 100 at a 15k group coaching price point. That is $300,000. Now we are talking serious numbers here. So even if they lost $20,000 on the front end, who cares when they go and make $300,000 on the next step. These are not just hypothetical numbers, these are real business models and I have clients pulling better numbers than these.

The most common business model: Free event > Front end offer of a 3-4 day event > backend offer of group or one on one coaching.

It's such an easy model to implement too, because you don't need to prepare anything the first time you sell it. Coaching happens in real time, you don't need to spend months recording a course or anything like that. Of course you either need to be a good coach or have coaches that work for you. Most of the speakers just have coaches that work for them to do the coaching sessions. I personally do the group coaching myself when I offer it, and I do have a one on one coaching offer with myself as well. Don't try to be like most speakers, try to be the best you can. People pay for you, they want you. Make an offer that you're comfortable with that gives them access to you.

Here are some examples of what you can sell on the backend that are proven to convert:

One On One Coaching

This should be your most expensive option as it has the most access to you. In my one on one coaching I provide 1x 45 minute call per month with me for a year, access to me via Telegram for instant communication and reviews of any material they have produced, years worth of fortnightly or weekly group coaching & a few other courses and materials. I price this at $30,000. I advise you to price this based on either a total amount of sessions or a period of time. Mine is a yearly coaching program so they have 12 calls to use in the year.

Group Coaching

Group coaching should be small groups if they are paying a high ticket price. If the price is something like $297 a month, then that's a free for all and so be it. But if they are paying $10,000+ per year and upfront then it shouldn't really get to over 50 people. The more people the longer the calls should go for. I offer mine weekly, but you can do fortnightly and structure it in a Q&A style whereby you coach the clients based on what they need help with in real time. I do mine weekly and keep it to under 20 so they are usually an hour long, it is between $10-15,000 per year. You can consider making this a monthly membership instead of a 'pay in full' price.

Recurring Membership

Recurring revenue is really helpful for cash flow and allows you to plan your next month's revenue and hire or make decisions accordingly. Any type of membership you can add to your business will greatly help. It might be a simple $97-297 a month membership for access to an online course or monthly Q&A calls. Get creative with it, and again this is optional as a downsell for those that couldn't afford your higher ticket group coaching or one on one coaching

And here are some front end offers (you can also use these as backend offers)

Short Term Specific Goal Mentoring

This can also be used as a front end offer. Essentially how this works is if you have a specific skill or goal you can help someone achieve in a certain amount of modules or weeks then you can package that into a program. For example when I started out one of my first offers was an 8 week program that would take someone from never having done an event or running ads, all the way to running their own ads and their own events. This was priced at $1,995 when it launched and I would advise that price for 8 weeks.

This is a very popular choice and a great seller. The beauty about this too is you won't need to spend much time recording a course. You only need to be one week ahead of the students the first time you do it. You can launch it as a first time BETA program. Have week one prepared, do a live group call each week and record it. That recorded group call then gets added to your program as well, and by the end of the first time you run it, you now have it all made. For someone that has nothing to sell I would start with this, because you could offer it today and make it work. All it consists of is one group call with you per week for 8 weeks and lifetime access to an online program that guides them through what to do each week. Sell this as either a front end or a backend offer, I usually do it as a front end offer. This also gives your students more time to get to know you and embrace your process, which will naturally give you a better opportunity to offer higher priced group coaching or one on one coaching.

This is a specialist offer, you are holding this 8-12 week program to help them get a specialist skill. So you can charge more than $2,000 but for the first time you do it, sell it at $2,000 and then increase to $3,000.

A Retreat

This one is one of my favorites and will be one of yours too if you like leveraging your business to fuel your lifestyle like me. Essentially you are hosting a 3 or 4 day retreat at somewhere like a getaway location with perhaps 10-20 students. It means you get a little business holiday, the people that buy get a business holiday and they get to claim it all as a tax write off! Perfect for both sides.

At Rockstar Speaker, we offered a retreat as our front end offer. You can use our offer if you like. We charged $5,000 + tax, and included: 3 days of the retreat, 3 nights accommodation at a 5 star resort, breakfast included each day, bring a guest for free, lunch included each day. Most people don't include accommodation, this is up to you but if you don't then just decrease the price. Essentially we wanted to make it a no brainer. My advice is to make your offer as much of a no brainer as possible to take all the excuses of not buying away. All the person had to do was pay for their airfares, everything else was covered. As a front end offer $3,000-$5,000 is a good price depending on what you are including, as a backend offer you could charge $10,000-$25,000 for your premium clients.

2-4 Day Event

Probably the most common front end offer is some sort of premium event for $3,000-$5,000. This can be 2 to 4 days. When I went to JT's first event it was two days and then the Dream Team event was for four days. So you can sell events from events. The difference between a retreat and an event is that there are more people at an event, it is less personal. Similar to a free event you will make an offer to your next step. These are usually local instead of at a special location and you don't pay for any food or accommodation.

Online Courses

Online courses were all the rage, however I don't love the model. They are usually a low ticket item like $697-997 and they take so much time for you to film it and record it. Low ticket, lots of time, hard to make profitable. I avoid selling online courses at events generally. It's fine to have an online course on your website or offer it via email as a follow up downsell option but this is not a high margin offer and you need to sell lots to make proper money. Also people procrastinate and use it as an excuse that they haven't finished their course so they can't sell anything. I'd much rather you use the 8-12 week mentoring model than a standalone online course.

Done For You

If you are in an industry where it makes sense to offer a done for you option, these are also great sellers. There is more involved on your end with costs and time and staff so tread with caution, but if you can do it, go for it.

Overall

Overall you want to consider the best options for you based on what your revenue goals are, what your ideal business model is, how many people you can realistically take per option and what you want your business to look like.

I advise that you do not do 'launches'. Some people love to launch their programs on specific dates and end on specific dates. I get that this will help you cater the content, but there is really no point in this day and age to not make an evergreen option. Otherwise you are shooting yourself in the foot. If your launch is December 13th, you literally can't advertise or take on any clients during that time until you are done and ready for your next intake. You are missing out on revenue. I make all my programs evergreen which mean people can join at any time because the group calls and the coaching is tailored to those that attend live and have their questions in real time. It doesn't matter what day they start or end! This is really important, don't waste your time with launches and specific dates, make it evergreen. Obviously the exception to this rule is when you have an in person 2-4 day event or retreat.

Also sell it before you create it. There is no point spending all your time and energy creating a course or a program, without selling it first. What if there is no demand and what if you can't sell it? Schedule in a free event, make your offer, sell your offer, if they buy, go and create it you only need to be one week ahead of the audience, and then rinse and repeat. You'll actually make it quicker this way because you have a deadline now and you're motivated because you got sales and you will make it better because you have the students there in real time to guide you on what they need next.

If you're struggling to come up with an idea for what to sell here are some simple options you could do today

Free Event > 3 day retreat > group/one on one coaching or 8 week group

Free Event > 8 week group mentoring > group/one on one coaching

Free Event > 2 day event > 4 day event > yearly or group coaching

Free Event > Done For You or Done With You for a specific time frame > Recurring offer

Even if you choose to do a retreat or an event, you can make the content after you sell it the first time. You set the date of the event at least 3-4 weeks after you sell it. Then you have 3-4 weeks to create the content and structure the days.

Remember your business model is extremely important so that you can maximize your revenue opportunities, spend more money on ads, get more people through the funnel and ultimately help more people with whatever you are helping them achieve. And finally understand that your business model will change, in fact you may find yourself offering all of these things at different stages of your speaking career. For me within the first two years I think I have offered everything except the recurring membership (not included recurring done for you options) on stage. Try things out, test them and see what works best for you.

This section has been all about understanding the business behind the platform speaking industry. Hopefully this has given you an insight into the numbers, the model, what to expect and how to approach different types of events. Most get dismayed because they do not understand the model and structure first and they skip right to the part about speaking, which is the fun sexy part, but without the numbers and without a solid structure, your speaking will only take you so far. Understand the business first and then we can create presentations that not only inspire and educate, but actually convert into sales.

12

How To Put Butts In Seats

If you have heard me speak before you will have heard me say that the first six steps of becoming a great platform speaker are all about marketing and the seventh step is the actual speaking. Although I don't recommend that you be the marketer that implements the advertising, there is another side of marketing that you do need to be responsible for. There are two types of marketing, there is the technical implementation which is all about actually doing the techy set up, this is something you should outsource to either me and my team or someone else. And then you have the creative marketing, which is about having marketing ideas such as titles, angles, hooks, names. You should be in charge of creative marketing. You are the entrepreneur, you are the speaker, it is your ideas that will make it work. Every one of the most successful speakers and even entrepreneurs in general that you see are also expert marketers. Grant Cardone - expert marketer, Tony Robbins - expert marketer, Elon Musk - expert marketer, the list goes on.

Most people take the lazy route and either have someone in their staff do it or ask their technical marketing company to come up with names and ideas. This is the most counterproductive action you could take. No one is going to care more than you and no one is going to know more about what you do than you. It's your business, not someone else's so take responsibility.

We have already covered some of the marketing principles throughout, however the main marketing principle is about your messaging. Your messaging is the main part of creative marketing.

Identifying & Acquiring The Right Audience

Earlier we covered the difference between warm and cold audiences, the next question to ask is how do you find the right cold audience for you?

This comes down to messaging, which I cover in depth in my other book all about marketing. Essentially you need to ask yourself what is the promised result of what you do? You want to sell the event as you would sell your offer. For example when we ran Rockstar Speaker, we also sold Rockstar Speaker Retreat at the event. It was congruent. Start with the end in mind. Rockstar Speaker is also an attractive title because they are both tangible words that people can understand and aspire to. It's when you use "woo-woo" words like "manifest your inner child and follow your destiny to the promised land" where it can get a bit too much.

If you are doing a free event with you as the only speaker your headline is everything. They aren't coming to see you, they are coming to get the transformation you are promising or learn more about the skill you are teaching.

If your event is with a celebrity or a drawcard that people will come to see, that's when you can get away with more of an edgy or broader title because they will come for the celebrity. For example 'Adapt Or Die' may not mean anything, or in fact be seen as too broad, but because we had Mark Bouris there it was instantly associated with a business frame for the event. So the broad term was now seen through the lens of a business audience.

You want your name to make it very clear either directly or indirectly who the event is for and not for. 'Rockstar Speaker' says it all in two words: you want to be a speaker or are one and you are not anyone else such as a tradie, or a builder or an accountant. 'Adapt Or Die' indirectly tells you it is for someone who wants to be able to improve their business despite the current circumstances, and the event is not for someone who gets offended at having a slightly edgy, in your face, title.

It is just as important to alienate the audience that isn't perfect as it is to attract the right audience. In doing so you will actually be even more attractive to that perfect audience. It's like an exclusive restaurant. If you can only get in by booking 5 months in advance and paying $1,000 up front that tells you that it's not for everyone, which means you attract a certain clientele. The minute you make that restaurant readily available with no wait times and no payment upfront, it loses its aura and attracts a different clientele.

The biggest mistake I see with people trying to identify their audience is by saying that they can help everyone and anyone. No you can't! The second you try to talk to everyone, is the second you talk to no one. Your messaging has to feel like you are talking to one individual person and one person only. It's the difference between an ad that says "we can help restore your body's vitality" (what does that even mean!) compared to an ad that says "we will restore the balance in your gut so that you no longer feel sick" compared to an ad that says "find out how to remove IBS for good, even if you think that you have tried everything to fix your gut". We go from way too broad, to somewhere in the middle, to very specifically handling an issue. The more specific you can get with your language the better.

In creating a name for your seminar I want you to remember this key point: Sell them what they want, give them what they need.

Read it again, highlight it, write it down.

As entrepreneurs we generally fall in love with our process. The thing is, a cold audience that we need to educate has zero idea about our process, and to be frank they couldn't care less about it. They just care about what's in it for them, what result can you provide them. It's like when you go buy a nice meal, you couldn't care less about how it is made, you just care that it tastes good. Same thing here. Don't waste your headline and your event name by trying to sell me on your process before I even know what you can do for me.

You know that the person needs your process, but all they know at this stage of their life is what result they want or what problem they need fixed. That's it. It's what we call market sophistication. And generally speaking the majority of your audience will be a low level market sophistication. That means, you need to educate them on what they want first, that you can actually help them achieve what they want, why they need to do what you're suggesting and then and only then can you introduce the methodology with which they can achieve the result with.

For example, in my events I sell a done for you marketing package for speakers. Almost 80% of my seminar is about marketing and 20% is about speaking. My ad to get people to even care in the first place usually has the headline 'do you want to be a speaker?' What do they want - they want to be a speaker. What do they need - they need the marketing engine that allows them to do as many speaking events as they want without the need to rely on anyone else hiring them or finding them. Do you see the difference?

If I marketed the event as 'a marketing event for people that want to be speakers' it would attract a much lower number of people and more of a curious crowd rather than a serious crowd. I say that because for someone to be interested in an event like that they would most likely have already been to quite a few seminars and have some level of knowledge by now, which tells me they could be procrastinators or freebie seekers - not my ideal audience.

Once they come to the event that is when you give them what you know they need to actually achieve results. It's all about mini steps of compliance. You can't ask them to marry you on the first date. You ask them first to sign up for the event because you have something they want, you remind them to come to the event, they then turn up and give you their attention, the longer they stay the more attention, the more investment they are giving you, then you can make your offer.

Create your event name based on the result and on these principles above. You can always change it later. It can be short like two or three words or it can be long such as: "How To Achieve A 6 Pack In The Next 60 Days." So long as it is clear, and the result is defined.

Advertising the event

Now that you have your title for the event we need to get sign ups!

This is what I specialize in and if you would like us to do this for you, you can reach out via my website ethandonati.com or you can attend any of our programs or events.

The first thing you want to do is create a landing page for your event. I suggest using Clickfunnels for this. I won't go into how and what to include, I have plenty of resources and events that go into this.

Once you have your landing page you need to send traffic to it. Use Facebook & Instagram ads as your main source of traffic. This is where I get most of my registrants. Optimize for 'Conversions' set your conversion as the confirmation page, create videos and images that advertise the event and go live.

If you are confident on video you can also use Youtube if you wish.

For any celebrity event I also recommend getting an Eventbrite page up as you will get some additional sales there.

Again the majority will come from the ads that you run.

How much should you budget on advertising?

This is a classic question, and the answer is that there is no black and white answer. You need to work it out backwards otherwise you are just guessing. Let's say it costs you $20 per registration and on average 20% of people show up, that means you are paying $100 per person in the room. Work out how many people you want in the room, plug in your numbers and that's your budget.

After they sign up, you need to remind them to show up. You can do this with email marketing and text marketing. For emails I use Convertkit, and you want to set it up so they go out automatically. Ensure one email goes out instantly upon registering, and then I have on average four emails that go out about 3 days apart from each other. These emails will resell the person on attending the event, explaining what they will learn, who the speaker is and why they should care. They act as a preframe.

A preframe is a piece of information that a person sees before they come to the event or watch your webinar or buy your program. It needs to get them excited and it needs to act like a movie trailer. You are giving enough excitement for them to actually care enough to come and watch the movie. Preframe material can be educational about what they are going to learn, it can even be a little tip, it can be video content, it can be testimonials etc.

My emails are usually email 1: confirmation email, summarize the details. Email #2: what they can expect at the event & inviting them to invite a friend. Email #3: written content that gives a sneak peak to what we will cover during the event. Email #4: why they should care about the speaker & some testimonials. Then leading up to the event I will send a week reminder, a day reminder and if it is an online event an hour before and time of reminder too.

For text marketing I will send two texts out. One 24 hours before the event and one about 20 minutes before for online events. For in person events it is usually 3 days before and the day before. A simple text with the times, locations and name of the event is all you need.

Finally if you wish to really maximize show up rate, you can also call the registrants. Have someone else call them and remind them about the event, this does help. It is optional however.

This here is a quick cheat sheet guide on advertising your event. It requires a lot of skill and experience which is why I do not recommend you doing your own marketing for the event. You should only take on the role of speaker & promoter/producer. If you would like to learn more about the technical marketing side of things or have us do this for you, please get in contact.

Preparing Your Messaging With False Beliefs

One of the main concepts that I teach is about understanding the false beliefs of your audience. This is something that was popularized by Russell Brunson. When people ask what should I sell? What do I speak about? What do I charge? They don't really have an offer problem or content problem, they have a customer knowledge problem. They don't understand what their audience wants and what they need. If you understood their false beliefs, pain points and problems you would know exactly how to talk to them and exactly what to sell to them.

Essentially false beliefs are a belief your audience holds about something to do with what you have to offer or even about themselves that is false. In fact, becoming a great speaker that can sell isn't about the information you are teaching, it's about helping them shift their belief system.

Think about it, when we are born we are a blank canvas. There are no beliefs, norms or what we deem 'acceptable behaviors'. From a young age though, what do we see? We constantly receive information. This information biases our behavior, teaches us what is right or wrong, teaches us what most people do, teaches us to conform and all of these different stimuli such as our parents, our friends, family, the media, our teachers all form to create our belief system. But who is the one making sure that what we are learning at this young age is actually the right belief system for us? In most cases, it's not. Chances are, somewhere along the line you had to shift your belief system to even want to get into entrepreneurship. Some of you may still be at that crossroads now - do I stay at my 9-5 job, do I start a business, do I try to do both? Shifting people's beliefs systems is the key to great marketing, great copywriting and high converting presentations.

Before we can shift belief systems we have to be aware of what the beliefs are in the first place. They are similar to objections in some instances, but an objection is usually a reason that someone gives you for not buying, whereas a false belief can often go undisclosed and sometimes the person is unaware they are operating with these false beliefs as they usually are taken for granted.

In a presentation you need to predict the false beliefs of the audience and when they will come up in real time during your presentation. Whereas in a one on one conversation you can address them specifically to that one person. Hence why the presentation style is harder to get right, you need to address as many as possible to the wider audience.

We can categorize false beliefs in three different categories: Vehicle, Internal & External.

Vehicle False Beliefs

Firstly, what is a Vehicle? A vehicle is something that helps someone go from where they are now to where they want to be. For the purposes of a presentation the vehicle is firstly you. You are a vehicle, the audience has to want to work with you in order to buy from you. The second vehicle is your methodology. When identifying your methodology consider this:

Pretty much every single offer in the world directly helps the buyer with at least one but most of the time all three of these aspects either indirectly or directly of their life: Health, Wealth and or Relationships. Firstly identify which of these three aspects does your offer focus on mostly? Let's say it's wealth. Well to find your methodology you need to create a sub-niche within the category and within the niches of that category. This will help get your message extremely specific. For example, let's say we are in real estate. So the category is Real Estate, a niche of improving your wealth, but there are many strategies within real estate investing such as: fix and flip, rentvesting, multifamily investing, buy and hold - the list goes on. These are all sub-niches. It's no longer enough to differentiate just by saying I help you with real estate, you have to own a sub-niche, you have to be a specialist of sorts to increase your conversion rate. Now if these sub-niches are also not specific enough, i.e. if we take 'fix and flip' there are a few people claiming they can help with this. You then need to give your methodology a name that signals how it is different to the other fix and flip experts. By all means you can still try to start off a little bit broader and hold a fix and flip seminar but then you will need to rely on you as a vehicle to sell, because chances are the audience has options.

So now you need to do this exercise for whatever it is that you sell in order to find the false beliefs. Let's say we chose Fix and Flip as our sub-niche of the real estate investing niche within the wealth category. To find the false beliefs go back up the tree. Consider this, if you went down the street and spoke to someone about how to build your wealth, chances are they will have lots of ideas about how they can do that: they can start a business, they can invest in stocks, they can invest in crypto. This is at the top wealth level. Well, guess what these are your first beliefs you need to address. You need to have an argument as to why real estate is a better vehicle than all of the other wealth vehicles out there.

Once you have done that, then you need to go down the tree. Let's say they now agree that real estate is the best way to build their wealth, now they need to know what kind of strategy is best, chances are they also have false beliefs about how to buy property and how to invest. Your next set of vehicle false beliefs are the difference between your sub-niche, in this case fix and flip, versus the other sub-niches, in this case buy and hold, multifamily, rentvesting and so on. These are the questions you need to preempt and address in your copywriting, in your advertising and in your presentation.

The other way you can find out more false beliefs you will need to overcome is by searching for complaints. Online Google Reviews, reddit forums or elsewhere, search some of your competitors in the industry and find out what the main complaints are. For example in my industry digital marketing there are common ones: "I've tried it before but it didn't work" or "I've been burned before" or "marketing just doesn't work for my industry". These are some common ones that I see. The funny thing is that most people think that their problems are unique and only relevant to them, in reality many people have the exact same problems or really perceived problems, and the solution is very simple they just have to get out of their way. That's the whole point of uncovering these false beliefs, to help people get out of their own way.

The vehicle false beliefs pertaining to you as the speaker and service provider are a little more straight forward. The most obvious one is about credibility. This can be addressed with proof, testimonials but even if you don't have these, conviction comes first. The way you speak gives you credibility. The others are more general: "you are too young or too old" "will you have time to spend on me or are you too busy?" "you are a (insert gender), you wouldn't understand my problems?" "I've tried this before, how are you any different?" Some of these seem vain but they do come up.

Your job is to identify as many false beliefs as possible in the vehicle section.

External False Beliefs

External false beliefs are more straightforward to understand, they are essentially circumstances that are perceived to be outside of the buyer's control which prevent them from buying. These are essentially the same for any industry and entrepreneur - time, money and resources. The main three are: "I can't afford it" "I don't have the time" or "I don't have the resources." We'll cover how to handle these later on, for now identify the right language your customers would use. I'm giving you the general language but they will work much better if you use the language your audience uses. I.e. instead of "I can't afford it" it might be "I don't have enough money to buy a property, don't I need to have at least $300,000 before I can buy anything?"

See how the much more specific language makes it far more relatable to what it is I am offering and that shows I understand the customer much better as well. Identify the false beliefs for the external category now in the language that your customers and prospects would use.

Internal False Beliefs

Internal false beliefs are similar to 'limiting beliefs' which you may have heard of. Essentially these are feelings and thoughts that your audience may hold about themselves that prevents them from buying. They need to be shown that people that were in their shoes were able to get results either through storytelling or case studies. Here are some examples of internal false beliefs: "It's easy for you because you are ____, but I am not like that" "I don't think I can do this" "I don't have the confidence like you do or like they do" "I am not destined for success" "I have never started a business before" "I've never done this before" "this seems too advanced for where I am currently".

The list could go on and on. As you do more presentations and come into contact with more people you will see all the different variations of limiting beliefs people have about themselves and you will be able to pick up on them. This will help you build a robust list.

Internal false beliefs are the most important because they are usually the most strongly ingrained in the person and they are less likely to consciously and overtly admit these to you. So you do need to tap into your spidey senses to pick up on these, predict them and pre-empt them.

Now that you know what the false beliefs are, start writing out what false beliefs that you think your prospects will have for each category. Now let's dive into how we handle and overcome these. Remember you will use the false beliefs for every part of the process from the ads all the way to the presentation.

Handling False Beliefs With Stories, Anecdotes, Stats & Social Proof

Now that you have your list of the most important false beliefs for your industry and for what you offer, it's time to handle these false beliefs. If you don't handle and address them before they come up, then it is likely you will not get the sale. You don't need to address every single one, that would take a long time, but you may want to choose one or two to go deeper on in an ad for example. The times when you address multiple are during presentations and during copywriting on a landing page. It would be a good idea to rank your false beliefs from most important to least important so that you know what you need to handle. Do this based on the frequency with which you see these false beliefs come up, the more common ones are usually there for more people.

There are a few ways that you can address these: with stats and data, with personal anecdotes, with anecdotes about other examples, with metaphors, case studies and social proof. You can pick and choose which false beliefs you handle with which option but you want to have a nice balance otherwise if you only handle them with one methodology it becomes repetitive.

Stats & data is a simple one. You can find many research articles using Google Scholar or you can look up reputable journals to find articles about your topic. For example if the false belief you were handling was about why Facebook ads are better than LinkedIn ads you can find real stats and data about how the cost per lead is lower on Facebook and how the average income of users is actually higher on Facebook too. You can find stats for most of the false beliefs around vehicle.

Personal anecdotes should be used sporadically. These should be stories about you and your experiences that handle a false belief at the same time as making you relatable. You will most likely have a back story or an origin story about how you got started doing what you are doing and why you are now in the industry that you are in. Chances are, that story will be the most relatable story because you most likely went through challenges that your current audience are struggling with too. Your personal story is usually great for internal false beliefs. For example when I tell my backstory about my social anxiety that relates to people who may feel nervous about public speaking. The stories you tell about yourself have to be told for a reason, they have to handle a false belief. It shouldn't need to be so long, it may be only 2 or 3 minutes. Always ask yourself why am I telling this story, what false belief is it addressing?

Anecdotes using other examples are what I would call borrowed credibility. Essentially the logic is hey look if this person is doing this, you should too. There's only so much you can do to convince someone to take what you are talking about seriously. You don't want to have to justify logically all the time because that doesn't work. You need to show someone why their belief system is not correct and why they need to change it, instead of telling them. For example I used borrowed credibility when I discuss on stage why you should be a speaker when I am talking to business owners. Because it's something they usually don't even consider I need to show other business owners that also use speaking to further their business. I show examples of Steve Jobs getting on stage to give product launch events, Elon Musk on stage to demo the Cybertruck. So you see borrowed credibility is about using anecdotes from other areas or other people that you can use to help bolster your argument. It also makes a great ad and great video when you liken your process to other examples like this, it demonstrates great logic and evidence.

Metaphors are a great way to address false beliefs really quickly and seamlessly. Metaphors are used to show a visual understanding of what you are talking about. As most of us can talk about quite techy or advanced concepts, not everyone is going to understand everything you say. It's the same for when you make arguments, not everyone will understand what your solution or offer can do for them or why they should change their belief pattern around buying your offer. For example, to pre-empt the false belief or objection of someone asking me "why can't I do this on my own?" a metaphor I sometimes give is: "let's say you studied on Youtube, read books and attended seminars about surgery, now let's say you or your loved one had to undergo a surgery procedure, are you going to do it yourself or are you going to hire the expert?" This type of logic and metaphor can help people see the difference between what they are considering and what the right course of action is to take. Think about some metaphors you could use and which false beliefs you could handle with those metaphors.

Social Proof is the final method to use to handle false beliefs and objections. When people say they don't have any testimonials well the good news is you have all of the other options above which are more than adequate to help you sell. If you do have testimonials be careful as most testimonials are terrible. A testimonial shouldn't just be "hi my name is x and I made $" a testimonial needs to handle false beliefs, it needs to tell a story but it also needs to be short. The best testimonial to get is video, and if you want to play it in your presentation it should be under one minute. The testimonials need to be relatable, I need to be able to relate to the person. This means you need many types of testimonials with different people from different countries, ages and genders because you need to appeal to a wide variety of people. If I speak in Singapore I use more Singaporean testimonials. If you use all Australian testimonials they are going to say oh well it doesn't work here then. It doesn't work for people like me.

The first type of testimonial is a logical testimonial. A logical person wants the facts, figures and data. This type of testimonial tells you what result they achieved by working with you and has to handle an objection. A great question to ask your client before giving the testimonial is to ask them "in 45 seconds or less can you explain where you were before you met me and where you are now?" This will generally give you a great logical testimonial that you can use. The 'where you were before you met me' will help them naturally speak about a false belief. For example they may say 'I have tried all of these other marketers before (handling false belief) but Ethan was the first one who got me 400 leads in 2 months (tangible result.)'

The other type of testimonial is an emotional testimonial. These appeal to those who are more in tune with their feelings and want to feel a connection and to be moved rather than just facts and figures. Here you want to set up a zoom call with your client and ask them to share their experience. You can ask open-ended questions and focus more on the feelings. I.e. How did you feel working with us? What were some of the surprising parts? These kinds of questions allow the client to open up and share their experience. You then clip out a minute of it to use in your presentation.

Overall with these options you should be able to handle 20-40 false beliefs at least during your presentation and you should be able to easily integrate this content to make ads and landing pages as well. This is vital to crafting a presentation and advertisements that convert. We do also help with this part of the process if you require.

If you are having trouble with headlines or what to call parts of your offer, keep in mind to also use the false beliefs that you find. These are literally used for everything. For example if some of the false beliefs are things like "I've tried marketing before and it didn't work" and "I don't have time to spend on this right now" then my headline could be "How to make your marketing work for you with only 30 minutes per day" this handles both false beliefs.

For the real estate example if two of the false beliefs were "I think real estate is risky" and "I have never bought a property before" a headline could be "How to buy your next cash flow positive investment property even if you are a complete novice"

Play around with your false beliefs and make some great headlines. This same method can be applied to create the items in your offer when you sell. I.e. "the 3 step mini guide to buying your first investment property regardless of your age, income level or expertise." I use this for everything, and I advise you to do the same. Take this seriously as it will make everything else so much easier.

13

Speak Your Way To Millions

The final hat you will put on is that of the speaker. You as the speaker is where it all comes together and culminates into one presentation. In fact if you don't put on your own events then you will really only need to focus here and on the false belief section. This is where it is showtime, when you get the mic, you are the authority on stage and you get to close.

This section isn't going to be about technical ability. I'm not teaching you how to project your voice and how to pause at certain parts of your speech, these are things you learn by observation. They are also things that don't necessarily lead to conversion. They may lead to an engaging presentation but I am more worried about conversion. If you really want to learn all that kind of stuff go to toastmasters. You won't be able to close but at least you will be able to be a polished speaker. You have to be ok with the fact that the more polished you are, the worse you will actually do. So many speakers focus on being perfect, wearing the perfect clothes and saying the perfect words. That doesn't help, you want to be imperfect, you want to be raw and authentic. Less thinking, more doing. You have to get out of your head, like a flow state in sports, you need to be in the zone. Once you're in the zone nothing feels forced, everything feels natural and you are performing at a peak level. Choose - do you want to be profitable or polished? This section will make you the former.

As the speaker, you need to protect your energy. You need to be able to put yourself in the best position to succeed, whatever that means for you. If you have been in athletic competition you probably have enough data points to know what you need to do before a match to perform at your peak. For me I always thought I had to be focused and serious before playing tennis and then I realized that only made me stressed out on the court. Instead my best performances came from when I was jovial and joking before the match. This is the same with speaking. You need to find the best mental state for you to perform.

There is one category above my jovial state and that is my angry state. I've always had this level of unwavering and unapologetic tenacity that I could go to in any competition, but in speaking I really didn't know how that would translate. If you have watched The Last Dance about Michael Jordan you would have seen how there are instances that made him get angry and competitive and those games would be his best. He would even make up things in his head that someone else said about him just to give him a fire for the next time they matched up against each other. That's the same feeling as what I get on occasion.

I remember in Rockstar Speaker after the first event I walked off and apologized to the team because my performance was crap. They all didn't know what I was talking about and thought I did great, this was the first time they had seen me speak so they didn't know what I was capable of. So then we get to the next venue the following day, and this anger has eaten at me for 24 hours now. I get on stage, blast it out of the water, I walk off and they say "Oh shit, that's what you meant." My state of anger, but controlled anger, is what gets me to my best performance usually but it also can burn me out if I rely on it too much, so that is why I am most often in a jovial state before the event. You need to find your levels and what state will be sustainable for you. Protecting yourself might mean avoiding certain people before the event, avoiding your phone, eating certain foods or even not eating certain foods. This is especially true for longer and in person events. Online you can really get away with anything, in person it requires a lot more energy.

Cherie had a great quote when she was coaching me: "as a speaker you want to be speaker fit and content rich." Essentially what this means is you better be prepared not only vocally but also physically to be able to deliver at 100% energy for hours on stage. If you aren't used to it, it can take a while to get used to. I recommend keeping fit by running so that you aren't out of breath on stage after a few hours. When I stopped training physically I remember doing some events where I felt so exhausted after 3 or 4 hours, like my lungs were going to implode or something.

The second part of the quote is all about being ready at any time for any situation. You should have presentations ready to go for any circumstance. If I asked you to speak tomorrow for 30 minutes could you? What about four hours? A content rich speaker can shrink and expand their presentation to as short or as long as they need regardless. It's the same with the stories we mentioned earlier, you should be able to shrink and expand any piece of content into what you need. The best speakers don't just focus on what they need to get right, they understand that no matter what goes wrong they have it covered.

The slides may not work, the microphone might not work, the audience may be silent, your videos in your presentation may not work, the promoter may change your time from 90 minutes to 45 minutes, the list of problems goes on. The best speakers are prepared for all scenarios and are not worried if any of them happen because they are professionals and they know how to handle it. It's like when Joel Bauer had his whole presentation get taken down during his close, most speakers would stop the event and say oh let me check what happened, fiddle around for 10 minutes with the AV, call the hotel team to help fix it all whilst the audience is completely out of it and lost interest. The best speakers get on with it, act like it's as planned, and still get the result they came to get. The truth is you should be able to keep going without any slides. Maybe you have a whiteboard or an easel to draw on, maybe you have nothing but just your mouth, use it. Be ready things will go wrong, you saw in my events how many things went wrong. Most would get absolutely thrown out of the water with any small challenge that comes their way.

Lastly what Cherie also said that is pure genius is "the best speakers create a need where there is none." This has to be the most important part to preface what we are about to get into when discussing closing during presentations. When a cold audience comes to hear you speak they don't have a pressing need to buy your program, to get help with whatever it is, fix and flip, property investing, marketing, social media, health, whatever it is most of the time they are not entering an event with a massive need for something. If they had a massive need they would just search on Google and buy something, not be attending your event. Your job is to create the need where there is none. Hence why went through the different ways to reinforce your arguments and handle false beliefs, because that task there helps you build a need where there is none.

Now it's time for you to tackle the most difficult skill but also the most rewarding skill on the planet: platform speaking.

What Should You Speak About?

Funnily enough one of the first things you need to consider is what will you actually speak about? What will your topic be? What will the name of your event be?

If you already have a business or you have already spoken in public before then you'll have your area of expertise that you can rely on. The issue for you may be are you positioning it correctly?

If you have never spoken before and you don't have a business then you have a clean slate to start off with and you can almost mold your skills and knowledge towards an industry and topic that is more easily monetisable than others. Remember as a platform speaker you need to make a return from speaking otherwise you won't be a speaker for very long. By all means if you have some other interest or knowledge in topics that are not as easily monetisable you can still talk about them but as a keynote speaker, where you speak for a fee instead of speak to sell.

As I mentioned earlier the three main categories of any great offer are; Health, Wealth & Relationships. These are three conscious drivers for most humans in their day to day life. People would be intrigued and interested in anything that helps them improve in any of these areas. These are the categories that you will have the most success in selling. Where most people go wrong though is by choosing a topic that is process oriented instead of choosing a topic that is result oriented.

A result topic is: "How To Get 6 Pack Abs"

A process topic is: "Understanding The Macronutrients, Calories, Supplements And Dietary Requirements Of A Healthy Body"

Both are focused on the health space but the first one is much more marketable and will appeal to a wider audience. The second will still appeal to a certain type of audience but it sounds much more boring and therefore you will not attract the same amount of people to attend your seminar. You need to hook people in with what they care about first and what people care about is 'What is in it for me?' What is the result they can get from listening to you speak?

The process may be discussed in the presentation itself, but it cannot be the hook to get someone interested enough on its own. Sell people what they want (i.e. the sexy headline), give them what they need only once they have given you their attention (the process of how you get the result).

If you are still deciding what to speak about keep in mind the following. Any topics that are personal development related, health related and relationship related where the client has to do work in order to achieve the outcome you are teaching them about will be harder to sell. You will need to be a better speaker than average to sell these types of services if you are charging prices above $3,000. The good news is that the majority of platform speakers do sell those type of services so the model has definitely been proven.

However if you want a topic that will be easier to sell for higher prices and does not require you to be as good a speaker to begin with, I would advise playing in the wealth space. There are many topics in the wealth space that you can be proficient in such as property coaching, business coaching, marketing, advertising, new business opportunities, to name a few.

Why these wealth topics are easier to get sales with is because it is easier to justify logically why someone should buy from you. For example if you are selling a $5,000 property investing course you can easily justify to someone that if they just have one successful property deal then they stand to make substantially more than the $5,000 that they paid.

Business improvement related offers are even better because a business can measure how much more revenue you are adding to them through your services. It is easy to track and easy to show improvement compared to say personal development, relationships or health offers where the improvement may be more intangible. Selling to business owners is also attractive to them because they can claim it as a tax expense which means your price really isn't as high as what it seems.

If I was to advise someone starting from zero, I would say get really good at a skillset that can help people improve their net worth. Unless you have some kind of track record in property, stocks, crypto or other forms of investing, I would choose a business growth related skillset which could be consulting, marketing, advertising, SEO, social media advice, get really good at it and then offer this in your presentations. You want your skillset to be applicable to as large an audience as possible so don't aim it at only corporates or larger companies, make your skillset applicable to small and medium sized businesses. Once you start getting great results you can then use your success in business to sell business opportunity offers to the general public and from there you can really scale. All of these services have very low, if any, overheads for you to provide them, which means great margins for you as well.

You can also apply this logic if you already have built a successful business in another industry. For example maybe you have built a great trades business, why not create a presentation about how to start and grow a trades business and then offer either an online course, mentorship, coaching or done for you service providing to help others do the same? This is the kind of logic and thinking required to enter the space of the information and knowledge economy, whereby you are essentially selling your intellectual property and teaching others how you achieved what you did.

Finally, when naming events, aim to keep the event title to as few words as possible, as marketable as possible and as interesting as possible. The result should be clear in the event title because ultimately this is what people will see the most of. The name of the event will be in everything - the ads, the website, the copywriting, the emails etc. It needs to have a ring to it. Think about it like this - if someone was talking about your event to a friend would they be able to say the name of the event and get a positive reaction straight away or would it require more explanation?

When deciding on a name, you should also keep the end in mind. You need to know what it is you're selling. For example when we did the Rockstar Speaker free event, we knew we would sell the Rockstar Speaker Retreat. So by selling the audience on the idea of Rockstar Speaker before they even got to the free event it made it that much easier to sell a retreat with the same branding and the same atmosphere. You want the name of your free event and the name of the presentation to align with the name of your paid product or service. If you are having trouble choosing the name of your presentation, work backwards from the name of what it is that you are selling.

What I Speak About & How It Has Evolved

When I began speaking I honestly had no idea what my core concept would be. What I realised is that it will continually change until you land on what feels most comfortable. It's very unlikely you'll get it perfectly right the first few times. The reason being is that you most likely have lots of knowledge about a particular topic and the more you try to include that knowledge actually dilutes your overall message. Even for me now I change up slides before pretty much every single presentation I do. I am always adjusting, editing and changing parts so if you are a perfectionist this may unsettle you. You will never have the perfect presentation so you will need to be ok with that.

Your presentation needs to focus on one or at most two micro-learnings rather than many different core concepts. For example I could teach someone about: Facebook Ads, Funnels, Social Media, TikTok ads, Websites, Copywriting, Landing Pages, Selling One On One, Selling One To Many, Speaking, Google Ads, and the list goes on.

If I tried to include all of those topics in one two hour presentation to sell one product it would be way too overwhelming and also it wouldn't appeal to anyone in particular as it is a broad set of knowledge. Every single one of these parts of knowledge fall under the realm of digital marketing but for the most success you need to focus on one part per presentation and hone in on a target audience. For example if we take 'Facebook Ads' the presentation could be teaching Facebook Ads to business owners who want to outsource or it could to business owners who want to do it themselves or train their team or it could be to someone who wants to learn to start their own marketing agency or it could be Facebook ads specifically for e-commerce stores, etc. All of these use cases for the vehicle of Facebook ads attract a completely different market and require different messaging altogether.

When I started speaking I started off quite broad and focused on digital marketing in general. It was a good presentation but it had no real hook and no compelling offer. The presentation I did in Colorado was really a general digital marketing discussion with no target market in mind other than 'business owners' which is quite vague. It can work but it requires a presentation that speaks to all different types of industries which isn't easy to do at the start.

When I started getting much better results I made one simple switch. This switch was to focus solely on speakers. All of my marketing revolved around attracting speakers to my events where I would then teach them how to market as a speaker, how to produce their own events and how to sell from those events. I would teach them how to create sold out seminars. The content was largely the same (80% the same) with some industry specific content added in, the difference was now I had a specific audience which meant all of my messaging, headlines and hooks made it very clear who I was talking to. This reduced my cost per registration in marketing and increased my conversion rate when selling because now everything was congruent to just speakers.

Why did I choose speakers? Simply because my marketing agency had some great results with speakers in particular so I could leverage those to show more credibility. Plus no one else really specialises in the speaking industry so I saw that as a massive opportunity.

This topic is still a major part of my speaking to this day. How it works is this: the first time a new person sees me speak is at either a free online 2 hour webinar or a free half day event. At this event I teach them how to market themselves as a speaker and why being a speaker is the best way to grow any business. They will learn about online marketing, advertising, the speaking business and funnels for speakers. I also cover how to create a compelling presentation and offer as well. It may sound like a lot but remember the overall theme is focused on one core concept: creating your own sold out seminars. So all of the points reinforce the main overarching theme.

From here I offer a done for you marketing solution whereby me and my team build the funnel, ads and marketing campaign for their event which we also help create and even coach them on the best approach for their specific skill set. Or they can choose to buy a premium 3 day event that goes in depth on the whole speaking business model, walks them through doing their own marketing and gets them practicing speaking in front of a group. The 3 day event is where you can give away all the complexities of your knowledge as they have already bought from you at this point.

The main takeaways from the above example is to niche down to a specific audience. By focusing solely on speakers I still did attract other businesses too and my offer was much more applicable and compelling because it focused on a singular target audience. Anyone in that target audience walks in knowing that I am a specialist for their field which means I can charge more and command authority much easier.

As a speaker you also need to have multiple topics you can speak about if some of your topics do not appeal to a wide audience. As my first topic is all focused on becoming a speaker I also need other topics that can assist other industries, as my skills can really help any business owner.

Once I had success selling to speakers and coaches now I could revisit my initial beginnings of targeting wider business owners. Therefore I created my second main presentation which is all about funnel building and why any business needs a funnel. Again it is a two hour presentation which teaches them what funnels are, why they need one, how it fits into their business lead generation strategy and then I cover how to run social media ads to the funnel so that they can scale.

Focusing on the topic of funnels in this instance is more effective than simply saying 'digital marketing' because it is much more specific and focused on the core element of digital marketing that is applicable to basically any style of business. It is also something newer and more exciting than simply another 'digital marketing' offer which is completely saturated.

After the two hour presentation they can buy a done for you funnel build from me and the team or they can buy a 3 day marketing intensive event where we will teach them to do it themselves.

For this topic the important thing to note here is that the positioning of my offer had to be somewhat unique. To make it unique, focus on one element of the bigger topic and lead with that as your main hook. In my first topic for speakers the focus was in having a specific target audience, for my second topic I want a broader appeal so my focus is in a unique methodology that directly links to a result for a wide range of business owners.

How To Create An Offer

Earlier I covered some ideas of the best performing products and services to sell at your free event but before we go into how to make a great presentation let's cover how to structure your offer. During your presentation you will have what's known as a value stack, which is essentially all of the inclusions of the offer on one slide and given a total value price. A total value price is what each individual item is worth on its own. The total value price will be substantially higher than the bundle price that they get by paying on the day.

Remember the offer you make in a presentation should not be available anywhere else. It should be a unique offer only available for those that see you on the day, otherwise the value is greatly reduced and there is no point to buy from you on the day.

The most effective way to write out an offer and decide on all of the inclusions is based on the false beliefs we covered earlier. Take down all of the false beliefs of your offer that may come up and provide a solution in your offer to each of these.

The offer firstly requires a main core inclusion. What is the main item that they are buying?

In my example the main item they are buying is a sales funnel. A Done For You Funnel is the first element of my offer, it is the main element. Your main element should reinforce what the presentation was about and fulfill the need that you have created throughout your presentation thus far. I.e. My presentation is focused on why they need a funnel so the first thing I offer is a done for you funnel.

After the main inclusion you then have your supplementary inclusions to handle false beliefs and reinforce the value of the overall bundle. For example if I build someone a funnel, the question is usually: how do I get people to the funnel?

So my next inclusion is running Facebook/Instagram ads to get traffic to the funnel for a specific set of time. The next logical question is: who will write the content for the funnel and ads?

My next inclusion is: we will write all the words that go into the funnel and ads.

The next question people have is well what if I want to eventually learn how to do this on my own?

So my next inclusion is a self paced online learning course that includes worksheets, downloads, guides and blueprints so that they can learn whenever they like.

Finally we include group coaching for a couple of months and three one-on-one calls which handle the false belief of: 'what support will I get?' Or 'I am a tech dinosaur I need hand holding'

Each of these inclusions is given a value and then stacked on top of each other to show the audience what they are getting if they buy today, what it is worth if they bought any other day but today, and then you can reveal the lower price for buying today.

Overall you want to aim for around five inclusions in your offer, sometimes more depending on how tangible or intangible your offer is. The idea is to make your offer so attractive that they would feel stupid if they said no. The way to do that is by addressing all of the major false beliefs that you identify and then solving them with a portion of your offer that directly addresses each of them.

The way you position and frame your offer is also important. I would advise you include something for free in your offer to frame it as a free bonus for buying today. For example when I do my offer I start off by saying for all of you buy today I am giving you my $10,000 live group coaching classes and online course for free. I also have this program on my site and it clearly says $10,000 if they buy online. The key with this framing technique is that it is much more valuable to anchor a free bonus of something that is high value than it is to simply include it in the offer. People love to get free things. The other benefit is that if they do not really want the free bonus it won't dissuade them from buying because in their mind they are not really paying for it anyway, it's a free bonus take it or leave it.

This is also a key concept when it comes to selling events. If you are selling a 3 day event as part of your inclusions, it is sometimes better to have it as the last inclusion and say it is a free ticket. That way if they cannot attend the dates of the event they are not going to not buy because it is only a free bonus and the very last thing you have shown on screen. They want to buy for the previous inclusions anyway so it doesn't matter if they cannot attend the free event. If you did this the other way and had the event as the main inclusion but they could not attend the dates, then that will mean you will lose the sale.

Create your offer in a bullet point format and ask yourself which false beliefs are being handled and what benefits each item has. The bold lines are the inclusions and underneath I have listed false beliefs that may be handled. See my example below:

Free Bonus: Weekly Group Mentoring & Online Course ($10,000 Value)

False beliefs handled: additional group support, ask Ethan questions in real time, meet like minded people, learn at my own pace.

Done For You Funnel Build ($24,000 Value)

False beliefs handled: I can't make my own funnel, it will take me too long, what if I try and it doesn't work, I want the experts

Done For You Ads & Tech Setup ($6,000 Value)

False beliefs handled: I don't understand Facebook ads, I don't want to spend all my time making my own ads, I don't know how to set up the tech, I am a tech dinosaur, I want this all outsourced

Done For You Copywriting ($14,000 Value)

False beliefs handled: I am not a good writer, I don't know which words convert, I don't have time to write, I need a professional to increase conversion

3x One On One Calls ($3,000 Value)

False beliefs handled: What if I need additional support? How will you know my business without speaking to me? I need hand holding as I don't understand any of this.

BONUS: 3 Day Online Marketing Event & The Recordings ($3,000 Value)

False beliefs handled: Can I learn more for me and my team? What if I want to be able to do this on my own one day? I want to understand what your team is doing so I can monitor and be more educated. Objection averted: because it is a free bonus it doesn't matter if they can't attend, they are buying for the other inclusions of the offer anyway. The recordings of the event also mean if they can't attend live, they can at least still watch the replay so they are not missing out at all.

Total Value: $60,000

Today's price: $10,000

There is an example of one of my offers, value stack and the false beliefs behind each inclusion. Now it's your turn! Write out your offer line by line, what is the total value of each option, what is the false belief you are addressing, what bonuses are you including and why?

Presentation Structure

The structure and principles we will cover here I have learned from a number of sources and combined to create my own style. I learned the closing principles from Cherie, the structure initially from Russell Brunson, the delivery by watching Cherie & JT and later on I learned different ways to articulate myself from Joel Bauer. My own style has evolved over time but has been a combination of all of these sources.

The way I think about structure for the presentation is in three segments. You have the introduction, the middle and the close. But here's the kicker, every single slide is a close. You don't just close at the end, that's where most people get nervous, you close from the beginning.

In terms of getting sales the most important parts are the introduction and the closing part. The middle part, although it takes up the most time of your presentation, is actually relatively straightforward if you get the start and end correct.

For those that hire me to coach them this is a major speciality of mine, reviewing your entire presentation and breaking it down. I stop it every minute or so and tell you how to fix it, change, why it's good or why it's terrible. In my programs there are also video examples of these that show you in real time how to make the best possible presentation. It all begins with structure.

The Start

The introduction is extremely important because it sets the scene. Put yourself in the shoes of the audience. They have no idea who you are, if you aren't piquing their interest from the get go why would they waste their next few hours with you? You have to command attention and hold it but not only that, also anchor it so that they stay for the whole duration. And even then, they may stay for the whole duration but not take you seriously because of your behaviour at the start. Someone that gives off the vibe 'please stay until the end I need you to stay' may get people staying out of pity, but they aren't going to get buyers.

Here is what I recommend for events that you do on your own. Let's say your event is scheduled for a 10am start time. Logon at 9:50am and have one of your students or someone that works for you or anyone that can help out begin the event. Have them introduce you, get the crowd ready and get them engaged. They can be the personable and attainable MC of your event, to position you as the authority. You NEED to be the authority. It makes me cringe when I see speakers out and about conversing with the audience before the event starts, this doesn't help your sales it makes you look desperate and attainable. After you speak, go for it, but before you start you need to set a separation mentally and physically between you and the audience. I've seen people do this online where they login and start asking people where they are from and all of this casual small talk for 10 minutes and they lose all of their authority straight away. You've lost the game before it even started.

Then after they introduce you, you don't go straight on, you have a video that also positions you as an authority. This is what we call pre-framing. The MC and the video act as a pre-framing tool so that by the time you even open your mouth the audience already sees you as an authority and they are already in a mindset ready to engage with you. If you do not have an MC you just go straight to the video. If it is someone else's event, they will most likely have their own MC that can then play into your video anyway.

When you get on stage, I don't care what you say, I just care that you keep the authority. Which means body language & tonality. You should be taking up space, right in the middle of the stage using hand gestures, standing up tall, commanding the stage not shrinking from it. When you start speaking it should be in 'breaking rapport tonality'. A vocal skill I learned from Owen.

Breaking rapport tonality is when your voice projects downward, instead of projecting upwards which is how someone sounds when they are trying to please someone. Hype up the crowd however best fits your personality and style before settling into your presentation. It is not about what you say it's about HOW you say it,

You should aim to get them excited for the whole event or the whole duration of your presentation from right at the get go. I start off by interacting with them so that it is engaging from the beginning. We will go through the exact step by step after the breakdown of each section.

Other areas to keep in mind for the introduction are this: do not begin by saying who you are. The biggest killer of any presentation is by starting out giving your whole life story and biography. No one cares! You have to make them care first. Yes it is 100% important that the audience has a connection to the main character, which is you, just like they would in a movie. But even in a movie they don't tell you the backstory first, they give you glimpses, they hook you in, they emotionally capture your attention. And once they have it, then they tell you the backstory. Always ask yourself, what is in it for the audience? Why are they here, what are you giving them?

That's why I always say that most people focus on all the wrong things. Why do most procrastinate, why do they never get started, why do they get anxious at the thought of jumping on a stage? Because this is the internal dialogue: "my hair isn't in the right place" "my makeup is off today" "my nose is too shiny" "I don't like how my voice sounds" "my logo isn't ready" "my presentation slides are not perfect".

It's all ME, ME, ME. It's selfish. That's why most people never get anywhere because they are selfish. They don't intend to be, but it's the truth. We focus more on our bloody brand kit and our appearance than actually delivering amazing content that wows the audience. Who cares about any of those things. In fact if you are that worried about it here is a task - dress down as much as possible, have the most imperfect slides and then give your presentation. See how much the audience cares. I am living proof of this, my slides are all over the place, they have different colors, they are not fancy, there is no branding and I was doing these online in a Nike hoodie! All your audience cares about is what is in it for me. And the introduction is where you make it abundantly clear that this presentation is about THEM.

The Middle

As I mentioned, the middle is the most straightforward part. This is where most people are the most comfortable because here you are educating. You do need to apply the closing principles that we will cover later, but for the most part here you are educating.

It should be structured into three content blocks and each content block is centered around one false belief. We will get into exactly how to do this in the next section. The middle will be the majority of your presentation. If you have done your job in the intro then you already have the authority and your audience will remain hooked during this time. We then segway into the close where you make the offer

The Close

If you have applied the correct structure the audience should not be surprised that you are going to make an offer to them. You will have been closing from the beginning and you would also have been desensitizing them to the price from the beginning. Most have already decided whether or not they will buy, it's your job here to articulate your offer in an attractive and easy to understand way so that they now do end up buying. Most new speakers get nervous when they start the close, but you really don't need to be if you make the right moves.

The close should take about 20 minutes in a 90-120 minute presentation.

Although I have seen some speakers take up to 45 minutes. I don't recommend 45 minutes because this is where you can get audience complaints. 45 minutes is a LONG time for an offer to be made, and it drags on and on. If what you have to offer is so good you should be able to articulate it and sell it within 20 minutes.

The mistake most make is that when they reveal the price point they just end the presentation there. But in reality over half your sales will come as you keep stacking on different closes. You should reveal the price relatively early in your close so that you have enough time to justify the price and convince the fence sitters. We will go over some techniques for stacking different closes in the next section.

14

The Step By Step Masterplan Sequence

Now you know the overarching foundation, let's break it down step by step as to how to exactly structure your presentation.

Remember this structure is for front end events only. This is not for any premium 3 or 4 day events that you may do.

Step 1: Preframe & Capture Attention + Authority

Play the video, walk onto stage (or for online turn your video on), greet and hype up the audience, capture their attention. We covered this above.

Step 2: Main Hook

The second step is to have a slide with the main hook of your presentation. I.e. If my event is called Sold Out Seminars, that is my first slide. I might say who here is ready to hold their own sold out seminars?

Step 3: Teaser Content

This should take about 2 minutes, and should be a teaser about one particular lesson. This should shift their beliefs straight away about why what you are about to talk about is essential to their success. I talk about having an audience and about the two most important skills that they need. So I use this time to introduce the main elements and more importantly tell them WHY they need it. This is where you create a need where there otherwise may not have been one.

Step 4: Ask Them Questions

Here I want to reinforce that they are actively participating and not just sitting back passively listening. I do that by asking them direct questions that they then either write in the chat box or they write down on the piece of paper. I ask them why they came today? I ask them what they want to learn, what their goals are and why they haven't achieved their goals yet.

In an online event you want to read out as many as possible, say the name of the person and read out their answer. This engages them on a deeper level as everyone loves to hear their own name. It is important to ask one question at a time, instead of all at once, as you want to be in control and talk about some of the answers. In an in person event I ask some people to share their answer and I repeat it to the room. This is an easy way to gain authority with the room from the get go and I do not see anyone else doing this as a speaker.

Step 5: Set The Scene

Immediately preface what the event is about or more specifically what the presentation is about. If it is a full day event with a break, you need to tell them the structure of the day, what they will learn in each section and why each section is extremely important. Set the rules and expectations of the day i.e. turn off phones, stay muted, no distractions etc.

Step 6: Introductory Content & Opportunity

Now you can begin to get into some more of the meaty content. I would suggest here you introduce what the main elements are to your formula and what the most common mistakes are and what to do instead. This way you are also shifting beliefs, it's important to do this here. So for example for me I tell the audience here are the four elements to great marketing, and yet most people think that likes, followers and comments are the most important things. So I instantly reframe their beliefs around what most people think versus what the actual answer is. This also gets them hooked on the rest of the session.

I also usually do some content here that wouldn't normally fit in my main middle part but is very interesting and gets people intrigued. So I talk about neuromarketing for 2 or 3 minutes here too.

Step 7: Introduce Yourself

You should be 15-20 minutes in now and here is the perfect time to introduce yourself. Start off with your highlights, quickly show where you are now and what you have accomplished. Don't stay here too long though because it will sound like bragging and tall poppy syndrome will kick in. Quickly transition into your back story. Remember your back story should handle a false belief and should give us some vulnerability that we can relate to. It doesn't need to be a sob story. Once your back story is done, quickly jump back to where you are now and show the full transformation. So we start at the high point, we dip into the struggle then we finish with another high point. Then we transition from there out of the introduction. You can say something like 'this training is not about me, it's about you' or use a hook 'who else wants to achieve x?'

Optional: Hook To The End

At any stage of the intro you can also hook to the end. I.e. if you are giving something away you can say "for all of you who stay until the end you will receive X."

You can use a mission hook. I.e. "My mission for doing this presentation is to help 100 people achieve X. Who wants to be one of them?"

Re-hook them on the presentation throughout your intro. I.e. "This presentation is about helping you buy your next investment property, who would love to buy it within the next 90 days?"

Hooks can be used throughout the intro to get buy-in from the audience.

That is the completion of the introduction, now we move to the middle.

Step 8: Introduce Your Three Secrets

Here you have your summary slide of what you are about to cover. You create your three headlines for the main portion of your presentation. These should be your three biggest false beliefs. Here you are signposting the content. You want to put lots of value in the final one and then when you introduce all three you say the last one is the most important one, this also hooks people to stay until the end.

Here are some of mine as an example: "how to master cold traffic & never rely on word of mouth again" and "how to make high converting funnels that sell for you 24/7." Both of these headlines are based on false beliefs and link it to a solution they would want to know about. You should also use a why statement such as "why funnels and personal brands are the best way to grow your business regardless of your industry" again handling a false belief and introducing your vehicle.

Step 9: Price Marinade

This is going to make your whole life much easier when it comes to selling. This can be a very intimidating skill to pull off but once you do it a few times it will feel natural. Here you are pretty much telling the audience before you even get to the main part that there will be something to buy at the end. Most people close by waiting until the end to talk about payment, well if you do it at the start I find it becomes much easier to talk about it again at the end and everyone expects it. It's completely transparent and ethical.

A price marinade is a slide where you say, at the end of this presentation I will make you an offer to help you with all of this and it will be valued at $X. You enter the total value price there. So if the total value is $40,000 you write that number here. Then you do not just skip the slide and go quickly through it, you hold here and let it marinade, letting the audience already consider the higher price. Ask questions like, would you pay $40,000 for a complete marketing system?

From here we move onto the main content

Step 10: Your Content Blocks

Introduce your first content block and teach as you normally would about it. Remember the key is to handle as many false beliefs during your teaching as possible. The structure of your content blocks should be: quick proof that it works to preframe the content, main content, testimonial to show the impact of that piece of main content. You don't have to include the first testimonial before the content but the last one at the end of each content block is important.

Most people wait to show all of their testimonials right at the end during the close but by doing it this way where it is during the presentation you are helping yourself sell easier at the end and you are showing that each part of the process works. This is where you intertwine case studies, metaphors, social proof, data and stats.

You repeat this for your three content blocks.

Step 11: Transition Into The Sale

The transition between content and the close is an important area of the presentation. You want to take your time here because rushing it will lose it's impact. The structure is very simple once you try it a few times. You have the same slide with all of the three content blocks and you recap what they learned. Then you ask them to raise their hand or type yes in the chat box if they learned something new or of value. Then you ask them to raise their hand or type yes in the chat box if they would like to know the details of how they can work with you. This may sound intimidating (what if no one says yes) but most of the audience will say yes. This is a permission close and again it builds trust with the audience because you are not forcing anything you are being respectful of their time.

Step 12: Starting The Close

The first thing you need to do before you begin to explain the offer is to pre-frame the offer. You need to consider this as a completely new section so once again consider this as a trailer to the actual offer itself. For me I have a video testimonial that I play to begin my close. You don't need to have a testimonial, you might just preframe the offer by explaining some of the success you have had with it or how it relates to what you have covered during the presentation. Then your next slide should be a single slide with the logo or the name of the offer. For me I say today you have the opportunity to take up the Million Dollar Funnels Package.

THE STEP BY STEP MASTERPLAN SEQUENCE

Step 13: Explain The Main Offer

For your main offer you should have four or five main elements that make up your core offer. You want to allocate one slide per element because the close works better when you take your time and when the audience understands everything. When you try to put too much on one slide in the close it looks cluttered and confusing. Have one slide per element and sell that element as if it was the whole offer. For example, one of my elements in my core offer is group coaching with me. Most people just say "Hey you get group coaching with me and you get email and you get ads and you get funnels." Instead you want to sell them on why each individual element is important and valuable if that element was itself the entire offer. I would go into the benefits of that element and explain what it costs by itself, why it is beneficial to them, explain that it is with me every week, explain the importance of accountability, explain the importance of having a Q&A every single week, etc. This is all before I even move onto the second element.

You want to do this for each element but you also want to remember not to get into a monologue. Remain conversational and continue asking the audience questions during your close so that you keep their engagement. The biggest mistake people make in the close is all of a sudden they go from conversational in the main presentation to completely monologue style when explaining the close. Ask questions, for the example above I might say "who here would find value in having me coach them every single week and learn from others going through the same process?" This keeps it engaging and it will feel natural and not salesy.

Step 14: Handle False Beliefs Within The Offer

When you make your offer, each element may in itself provoke new false beliefs and objections, you need to handle these in real time during the presentation. They don't need to be slides for each one, you just need to remember to address them in the right parts. For example when I introduce the group coaching element I need to predict what objections and questions will come up. One of them might be "when are the group calls?" or "What if I can't make them live?" I address these during that part of the offer. There will be new questions and objections for each element so handle them after you explain the element each time.

Step 15: Social Proof Of Each Element

As you walk through each element of the offer, if you have social proof by way of testimonials or case studies for the individual elements, use them. This helps to sell the element on it's own. For example when I am explaining the coaching component I will show a testimonial of someone who just did the coaching and nothing else. The key principle here is to sell each part of the core offer as a standalone item, add whatever you think adds to the sale of that individual component. Do not obsess over the steps themselves, it is the principles you need to understand so that you can implement them in your own way.

Step 16: Value Stack

A value stack is where you have each line item of your offer on one slide with the full price next to each of the line items. This is how you get your 'total value' number that you see on most sales slides. Now some people will tell you to have a value stack slide after every single component, I think this is probably overkill. You definitely want to at least have a value stack after you have mentioned all of the components but other than that I base it off of the amount of time between components. If one of the components is quite a short two minute explanation, I wouldn't restack the whole offer. I have around three value stack slides during my initial core offer explanation.

THE STEP BY STEP MASTERPLAN SEQUENCE

What You Get...

- **Lifetime Access to My Million Dollar Funnels & Ads Training** ($6,994 Value)
- **8 Weeks Group Coaching** ($4,000 Value)
- **Ethan & Team Build YOUR FUNNEL FOR YOU** ($10,000 Value)
- **Ethan & Team To Create, Manage & Optimise Your Ads For An Entire Month** ($2,997 Value)
- **Ethan & Team To Write Your Copy For The Funnel, Ads & Emails** ($14,000 Value)
- **Ethan & Team To Automate Your Email Sequence** ($2,000 Value)

Total Value: $39,991

A Value Stack example

Step 17: Summarize The Result And Outcome Of The Core Offer

Once you have explained the final value stack, before you get into the price reveal you want to summarize the result and outcome intended for those that buy. This is useful because when you explain the offer for 15 minutes it's a lot of features rather than necessarily reminding them of the outcome. In this section you can use more testimonials of the entire offer such as other people taking up the offer and you can state the clear outcome and result that the buyer will be aiming for by taking the offer up. What is the outcome?

Step 18: I Had Two Choices

Here we start our descent into the price reveal. This is a strategy I learned from Russell Brunson called the I Had Two Choices Close. Essentially this is where you separate the audience and pre-justify your price point. An example of this in action is "I had two options, the first option was to make this extremely affordable and try to have as many people as possible join but that means I wouldn't be able to keep the same level of support and results that we want. The other option was to price it at a bit more of a premium and by doing so we keep it more exclusive and maintain our world class quality."

This allows the audience that resonates with premium offerings to feel like this is perfect and that your logic makes sense. It also removes the people who are not serious. Finally, it desensitizes them to the fact you will be making a higher priced offer than maybe they would expect. Remember you have also done the price marinade at the start so this reminds them of the price you said initially as well. Better to have this higher price in their mind and reveal a lower one as opposed to thinking they were coming to a free event and then all of a sudden have to pay $5,000.

Step 19: What Would It Be Worth?

The last step before you reveal the price is to ask the audience to reflect on what it actually would be worth to have your solution. Here you should also refer to the marinade price. I.e. "Would it be worth $40,000 to have one perfect funnel built for you?" "What would it be worth to generate 100 leads this month?" "What would it be worth to finally have a marketing system set up?" You can ask four of these kinds of questions and then you can transition into the price reveal.

Step 20: Price Reveal

With pricing you essentially need three prices.

1. *The Total Value Price.*
    This is the price you do the price marinade with. All this means is that

if you were to value each individual component of your offer what would it be worth? This will be your biggest number. It doesn't mean you charge this, it just demonstrates the value if they were to buy each component separately.

2. *General Public Price.*
This price is what you would charge if someone inquired on your website as opposed to being there on the day with you at the event. This is essentially your normal price.

3. *Today Only Price.*
The reduced investment price they will get as a result of buying today.

We have already used the total value price in the last step and in the price marinade. When you make the actual price reveal there are two ways I like to do it.

The first way is the safer way that most speakers use and I recommend this for beginners for sure. Here is how it works:

You mention that you aren't going to charge the total value price and you reveal the general public price. I.e. "I'm not going to charge you $40,000, in fact the general public price is $10,000."

Then you hold on to the general public price for a little bit. You can restate the offer or justify the general public price as a steal because of whatever reason you want to add in here. Then you reveal the actual price. "For those that buy here and now today you won't pay that price either, the price for those that buy today is only (insert the actual today only price)"

The other option is much more advanced and only recommended if you are directly making a money related offer where you can track how much they make from working with you. This is my favorite close and actually when I started dramatically improving my closing rates this was what I used.

Step 20 Advanced: Price Reveal With A Half Half Close

In this close you do not budge on your general public price, you just make it a conditional offer. The condition is they only pay the remaining amount if they make a certain amount of money from working with you. For example if the general public price is $10,000, a half half offer would be: you only pay $5,000 today and the remainder only if you make $50,000 within x amount of months.

This is a great close because you can keep the actual price and make both parties invested in the offer. You can also mention this in the close and refer to the fact that you both have skin in the game. Make sure to explain how this deal works because the natural question here will be well how do you track how much I make? You need to explain that this is going to be based on the honor system. You are betting that if they make $x that they will be honest enough to tell you and provide your bonus. You also have to make it clear that if they do not make the goal revenue amount that they will not need to pay the other portion of the price.

I have seen people do this with a $25,000 full price but you only put $5,000 down on the day and the remainder is conditional on a $100,000+ revenue result. This is a great close, hard to pull off, but if you can it lends itself to a lot more of a creative closing structure with a win win for both parties involved. Again only attempt it if your offer relates to making more money.

Step 21: Tell Them How To Buy

Now you have revealed the price, this is where your heart starts racing a lot more. This is also the time where the emotions and pressure if you are newer may overwhelm you and create mistakes in what you do or say. The most important part is you must TELL them how to buy. Seems obvious but it really is not. You need to really spell it out for the audience. Tell me exactly how to buy.

If you are online, you simply post the link in the chat box and tell them to click the link in the chat box. If you are in person I tell the audience that they can stand up and go to the back of the room once they believe this is right for them as long as it is before I get off stage. You can't just tell them once you need to tell them a few times throughout this part of the presentation. I will literally tell them, stand up and walk to the back of the room, talk to the team and they will give you the details to sign and then you can pay with credit card. I will even show them a photo of what the signup form looks like.

Step 22: Guarantee (Optional)

At this stage the audience knows how to buy and technically you could get your first sales now. Most of the time the sales don't happen immediately, they will happen after this point so here is where you want to understand where you are in the presentation. Essentially what you have done is you spent the last 90 minutes getting the audience to an emotional buying state, they are there and if you have done your job they will emotionally want to buy. Now that we have revealed the price, there is sticker shock and we now need to give them logical reasons to do what they emotionally want to do.

One way to start this is to use a guarantee. You need to be careful with guarantees depending on what you are selling. I do not recommend a guarantee if your service requires one on one time with you or additional costs such as required for 'done for you' services. If however your offer is a group coaching or an online course or even an event, then a guarantee may make sense and make it a no brainer.

Some guarantees could be a 30 or 90 day money back guarantee if they are not happy, these are pretty standard. For events you can make it so that if they don't like day 1 then they can refund. Anything that helps make it a no brainer and takes out the risk of participation is fine to use as a guarantee.

Joel Bauer has the best guarantee which is if you don't triple your investment after you make all the moves then you get a full refund plus $1,000 and you have up to 12 months to claim this guarantee. I don't necessarily recommend that, but you can pull this off because the client would need to prove that they made all the moves to be eligible so if they don't put in the work then there is no refund.

Step 23: Additional Logic Closes

Here you can continue to justify the price point using logic. You can do this by comparing it to alternatives, such as what is the cost of alternatives? How much does it cost to go to university to learn this? How much have you lost by not achieving this? How much will you continue to lose by not achieving this? What is the cost of inaction? What would you need to make the money back? How many more clients would pay off the investment? What is the worst case scenario v the best case scenario?

The principle here is to break the price down logically either using maths or logic based questions that allow the customer to justify in their own mind how they would make the investment back.

Russell Brunson also recommends telling the audience that they now have two options. Which is a continuation of the two option statement you made earlier. This way however you are saying "you have two options either stay the same or invest a small amount in your success to achieve ___"

Anything that breaks it down logically for the customer is what is great to go here.

Step 24: Fast Mover Bonuses

Once you go into the logic you will start seeing buyers move. However now you want to insert the straw that breaks the camel's back. That is the final inclusions of the offer. Ideally you have two or three fast mover bonuses for those that buy right now. These bonuses should actually be worth the whole investment on their own. They can be additional courses, additional support, one on one calls, whatever you like. For me I usually include a one on one call with me or three with my team. Sometimes I include a Facebook Ads course, it just depends on what fits with the offer. For example for an event I sell for $997 the core offer is the 3 day event. The bonuses are complementary to the event because an event is a live experience, what happens before and after the experience can they keep learning? No, so an obvious bonus is lifetime access to an online course that they can access anytime to start learning straight away.

Think about what bonuses you can make or already have at your disposal and then add these at this part of the presentation. You need to sell each bonus as a standalone item just like you did for the core offer and emphasize that this is for those that buy before you finish ONLY.

Once you mention all of them, restack the offer with your entire value stack that now includes the bonuses as well as the core offer.

Step 25: Review Entire Offer, Final Push & Reminder How To Buy

At this stage most people should be going to the back of the room. Here you do a last push that reminds them of the offer, justifies how reasonable the price is and most importantly you remind them to go to the back of the room or click the link. Tell them how to buy.

If tax is included or if it is a tax deduction/tax break for their business make sure to tell them too.

Step 26: FAQs To Finish

Even though you will see lots of movement and you might feel like everyone that was going to buy has done so, you'd be wrong! The FAQ's are the last part that you do. If you are online you could do this for 10-15 minutes just go through as many questions as possible, in person you want to limit yourself depending on how much time you have for the whole presentation.

Anyway the thought here is you have one slide per false belief and you handle the most important ones. I write out all the false beliefs that someone may have about the offer and potential questions they may have which act as a reason to not buy. Then I choose the most important 5-10 and make one slide per false belief and frame it in a question.

You can say "you may be thinking, is this only for advanced people?" or you can frame it as FAQ's: "here are some common questions we get about the program. #1 Is this only for advanced business owners or can beginners do this too?"

You address each question, and after each question you soft close. All that means is reaffirming their decision and intention to buy. You will be surprised how many sales you get from this part of your presentation especially for online events. For online events I recommend having a lot of these and just keeping on going until all of them are handled.

After this you say thank you and that you are looking forward to working with those that signed up and you are finished!

Keep In Mind

One thing I do want to mention is that if you see lots of people at the back of the room you ideally want to keep speaking for as long as you can. This is something I learned from Marshall Sylver, who said that as a speaker the sound of your voice on the audience is similar to that of a hypnagogic effect. Essentially the audience has trust and comfort in hearing your voice and as they are waiting for their credit card to be processed and to sign up, by maintaining the sound of your voice they remain in the buying state. If the room suddenly goes quiet, the vibe gets kind of weird. The energy is gone and that cuts the state out. This means some people may not buy and walk back to their seat.

Consider it for yourself if you are listening to music on a night out and then all of a sudden the venue goes dead silent, the entire vibe changes. This can and does change behaviour. It's the same thing for the events too. Which is also why you want to have music ready to go, the second you walk off stage. The music shouldn't be lowkey, melancholy or too relaxed, it should be a song that adds to the excitement and positivity. We are holding the state of the audience until the end of the purchase cycle.

The last main question I get is about the number of slides. The truth is the number of slides is largely irrelevant, it depends on your presentation style. I do recommend a slide per thought to keep it simple and easy to follow for the audience. This does mean you may end up with 200-300 slides for a 90 minute presentation. Especially during the close you do require a large amount of slides because you need to have one idea per slide and it has to be easy to follow. My current presentation has about 300 total slides and almost 100 are the offer.

The Principles Of Closing Throughout Your Presentation

Now that you have the structure you can be sure that your presentation will hit the mark. Following that structure alone will be able to get you sales and it will be able to create the perfect combination of education, inspiration and conversion in 90-120 minutes. The next step is understanding some of the fundamental advanced principles that you want to sprinkle into your presentation throughout the main content.

Trial Closing

Trial closing is asking for small bits of mini compliance. You're essentially asking the audience to say yes or agree with you in some way. When you think about it, a presentation is all about accumulating forms of small compliance that leads to the main compliance of buying from you. Trial closing should happen all throughout your presentation from start to end, it should become a part of your natural delivery. It can start off by feeling weird and forced but the more you practice it the easier it will be.

Cherie was probably the first person to teach me this and I didn't really get it because talking to people was foreign to me, but then I forced myself to try it more and more and I finally got it. Here are some examples of what trial closing questions are:

Is it ok if I share my method with you?

Who here would like to achieve more confidence in their life?

Raise your hand if you would like more clients this week.

At the start of your presentation you will ask safer questions like the ones above. These are pretty risk free questions where the obvious answer is 'yes' or 'me' or some form of agreement with you. As you go deeper into the presentation you may ask for even more compliance such as:

Who here would pay $20,000 to have someone do this for you?

Would it make sense to hire a coach instead of trying to figure it out on your own?

These questions are more focused around the sale as opposed to the first few which were more about general desire questions. This is what we mean by the presentation is what is closing for you, not just the end sale part. If you do trial closing all throughout your presentation you are literally closing the audience on just about every single slide! This needs to be a regular part of how you present. You can practice in your everyday life, just naturally try to bring some closing questions into your normal conversations, examples could be "does that make sense?" "sounds good right?" "Does this seem like a better option?"

Trial closing isn't just about getting someone to say yes 100 times, you'll seem odd if you are coming across like you're just trying to get people to say yes. It shouldn't be forced, it should feel natural. Also don't be afraid to ask a 'no question'. People need to be able to feel autonomy. Generally sales people just try to get the buyer to say yes all the time which takes away autonomy and results in lost sales. I like asking no questions straight away such as "have you given up on this year already?" and at the end "would it be crazy to think that you might get better results with a coach?" You don't need too many, but ask no questions as well to show that you are not just a robot.

Future Pacing

Future pacing is a technique to keep people interested to stay for the entire presentation. Sometimes it's just to have them stay ten more minutes, and then ten more until they stay until the end anyway. We need to get them interested to stay as the brain is lazy and otherwise may just say it's not worth the effort energy. This is extremely important for online events as the person has so many distractions around them anyway that it is that much more difficult to hold their attention for 90 minutes or longer.

We aren't asking for compliance like we are in trial closing, instead we are hanging a carrot so that they care enough to stay. For example, when we introduce our three content blocks of what we are going to cover we might say "and the third secret is all about _____, this is the most important part of the day" this future paces that they need to see the third and final content block. Other examples are saying that the day is structured as a progression so that we go from beginner to advanced content and it all leads into the next part. Similar concept and now we are managing their expectations by subtly saying that the advanced content they need is at the end.

Future pacing isn't just to have them stay until the end, you also want to future pace your offer. I do this quite early in the start around the price marinade section. For example you may say "At the end of this presentation there will be an opportunity for 5 of you to work with me directly."

Unlike trial closing where we want to do that throughout the whole presentation, future pacing needs to be emphasized early on in the presentation. Especially in the first 15-30 minutes there needs to be a few times where you are giving them something to look forward to. If there is no one staying until the end you can't make a sale!

Urgency & Scarcity

You may have come across these terms before as they are quite common in marketing. Urgency is basically answering the question why should someone buy NOW? A lot of people are very good at making an offer and showing the value as to why someone should buy, but they can't answer the question; why should you buy *now*? And if you cannot answer that question, you will get much fewer sales than you should.

Scarcity is essentially showing that there is only a limited amount of this and not everyone can get it. If everyone could get it, it would seem too available and you would seem too desperate that you just accept anyone. It's kind of like having standards.

Let's start with urgency. Out of the two, urgency is more important. In the structure of the presentation you'll notice we added fast mover bonuses.

This creates urgency. This answers the question of why should I buy *now?* Simple, because if you don't, these fast mover bonuses go away for good. You can have a countdown timer for the offer, so that once it expires the offer is done and you can also emphasize that the price goes up to the normal price after your presentation ends. The fast mover bonuses can be the most powerful, just make sure you really make them incredible.

Scarcity is a bit different and can be a slippery slope. Most speakers in the industry use this unethically. I wrote about this earlier in the book, how they just lie about numbers. They say things like this are only available for 10 people. That's totally fine if it's true. But if the truth is that 50 people run to the back and you accept them all then that's not a true statement. One way to have scarcity is by setting a limit to your offer, but it has to be real not fake. So workout what your limit would be, and then you can confidently say that number. That's one way to do it, however most people don't believe those kinds of statements. The truth is though, the fast mover bonuses also add to scarcity. Because the scarcity is actually that the bonuses go away after today. So just by adding that one element to your presentation you will be able to add both urgency and scarcity in an ethical way.

These usually happen during the call to action when you are making the offer but can also happen as a future pace too earlier in the presentation. Remember the whole point is to answer the question why should someone buy now? Why do they need to buy now? Couldn't I buy it later? If you don't answer these questions you don't get sales

Seed Planting

Seed planting is exactly how it sounds, you are sowing the seed that you do have paid programs. Essentially someone can't be surprised when at the end you are making an offer, If you find yourself getting comments such as I didn't expect you to sell anything, it's most likely that you didn't do any seed planting. The best form of seed planting is by leaving it as an open loop so that they fill in the gaps. For example: "in my coaching program we go a lot more in depth on this topic here" or "in my group coaching I help my clients complete their manuscript." It's an open loop because you aren't telling them that they can sign up to your coaching, you are just mentioning that you have coaching and you have clients that you do this with. This means they may even ask you, how can we join your coaching? If you get questions like that, you are doing great! This is how you get people to ask you to sell to them.

Seed planting should be done during the presentation but only needs to be done 2 or 3 times for maximum effect without overdoing it.

Seed planting should be done during the presentation but only needs to be done 2 or 3 times for maximum effect without overdoing it.

Summary

These techniques here are designed to make you a much better closer when you speak. There is some overlap between them but to summarize the main points so that you know the differences:

Trial Closing: This is about gaining compliance from the audience with small but obvious questions where the answer is 'yes' or 'me'. This should be done all throughout the presentation from the start.

Future Pacing: This is about making sure the audience knows the best is yet to come so that they stay longer. Ideally so that they stay until the end. This should be used 3-5 times in the first 15-30 minutes. I also recommend using this in the middle to set expectations. For example at content block number two I will even say ok so in ten minutes time we are going to cover how to do x, but before that we need to know how to do this. If I am ahead of time I also say, we're ahead of time and we only have 15 minutes left before we are done guys so let's lock in for these last 15 minutes (future pace), who here has already gotten massive value or learned something new today? (trial close).

Urgency & Scarcity: Answering the question of why should someone buy now? This is used in the close when you are making your offer.

Seed Planting: By the end of the core content the audience should already know that you have a premium program and they may even be wondering how they can get involved. This is without you even making an offer yet. Seed planting should be used 3-5 times during the main presentation.

What Do I Say For The Main Content?

Some people do ask what they should talk about in the main content. Now generally speaking you as the speaker and the expert will be best poised to make the content because it's your expertise that you are talking about. Remember to structure the three blocks around the three biggest false beliefs and you will naturally have content that does educate but also helps you sell. There is one principle though that you can apply to always keep you on track. That is what Russell Brunson calls The Big Domino.

The Big Domino is a statement. You don't say it in your seminar, but you structure all of your content to knock over the big domino. Once the big domino is knocked over, well just like real dominoes, the rest fall down. If they all fall down the audience buys. Here is how the statement works: "If the audience believes that X (your vehicle) is the best way to Y (what they desire), and is only attainable through Z (your offer), then they must buy from me."

You'll notice the emphasis is on belief. Your main job as a speaker is to shift beliefs first, then teach them how once they buy from you. You want to go back and make a big domino statement so that you can then assess your content based on how well it relates back to your big domino. You'll be able to naturally cut out or include different content when you have this direction.

For example one of mine would be: "If the audience believes that becoming a platform speaker is the best way to make their first or next 7 figures and is only attainable through Sold Out Seminars then they must buy from me."

Now when I build my presentation I am asking myself, ok how have I made sure that they know that becoming a platform speaker is the best way? Have I addressed the other ways? Have I shown the differences? Have I shown that it is possible for them to do it? I can ask if my content is in alignment with this or if it is just filler content that doesn't add anything to the main statement.

If you are having trouble with your main content this would be a place to start.

15

It's Your Turn

We've now covered the entire structure and principles you need to speak and close. Although it can seem like a lot of information and perhaps difficult to understand at first, it does become normal after you try it out. That is what we refer to as the speaker journey. You will constantly change your presentation, you will add things, you will remove things, you will adjust based on the real time questions the audience asks you. You don't need to try to get it perfect the first time or beat yourself up if you don't get a sale the first time. This is a skill that requires constant adaptation and transformation throughout your entire career. You'll need to change based on the context of the environment. For example during the COVID lockdowns as a speaker you had to address that, you had to position your offers and your seminars in a way that fit the times. You will always need to do that.

My best advice is to understand the principles first. The principles allow you to make your own rules and find your own way because you understand why it works, not just what works or how it works. Once you understand why it works you can create any presentation, you can improvise at any time and nothing can throw you off.

This industry isn't for everyone but for those that fully commit it may just be the most rewarding decision you ever make. Not just for the money, not just for the connections, not just for the celebrities and experts that you will open doors to work with but also for the internal fulfillment of being able to impact more people with a skill that most will shy away from. To do something that most won't ever get the chance to do and to do it as a career is something to never take for granted.

It really is like being a rockstar or an elite athlete in terms of the small percentage of people that make it and the big upside of what can be achieved just without the public fame and the pressure that comes along with such fame. I wish you success and maybe we will even share a stage one day. Get on stage like you were meant to. Don't just say one day, start planning right now. When would your first event be? What would it be about? Start making your presentation. Put the wheels in motion or else you may never get to it. If you have any inkling whatsoever to be the person on the stage, you owe it to yourself to give it everything and to start immediately.

Now if you want my help, if you understand the importance of having the right coach in your corner telling you what to do and helping you each step of the way then I have an offer for you. For reading this far it's only fair that I make you an offer now. Send an email to: admin@mymilliondollarfunnels.com with the subject line 'RE: No One's Coming Coaching' if you want me to coach you personally, tell me why you want to be coached and a bit about what you do or what your dream goal is. If I think that you are someone I can work with you'll be offered a coaching package that I do not offer anywhere else.

And remember, No One's Coming to speak for you, No One's Coming to put you on the stage, No One's Coming to learn it for you, build your presentation for you or sell it for you. No One's Coming to make you successful and no one is going to care more about your success than you. You've got to do it yourself.

IT'S YOUR TURN

Now go and do it.

If you loved the book tell us about it! Share a photo, story or post and tag @ethan.donati on Instagram.

About the Author

Ethan is the CEO Of Million Dollar Funnels and Sold Out Seminars, a TEDx and International Speaker, #1 Amazon Best Selling Author and a two time *Two Comma Club* Winner.

His experience in digital marketing has generated unprecedented results for his clients earning him praise from entrepreneurs all over the world.

He has co-headlined events with - and run ads and made funnels for - celebrities and experts including Seth Godin, Mark Bouris, Janine Allis, Naomi Simson, Eric Thomas & more

You can connect with me on:
🌐 https://ethandonati.com

www.ingramcontent.com/pod-product-compliance
Lightning Source LLC
Chambersburg PA
CBHW070251010526
44107CB00056B/2427